I0463191

Local Business

INSANE

RESULTS:

How Local Businesses Are Cashing In On Marketing Their Businesses Online

By Jason C. Maxwell

Copyright © 2011 **Jason C. Maxwell** All rights reserved

Local Business *InSane* RESULTS

Copyright © 2011 by Jason C. Maxwell

All rights reserved. No portion of this book may be reproduced mechanically, electronically, or by any other means including photocopying, without written permission of the publisher. It is illegal to copy this book, post it to a website, or distribute it by any other means without permission from the publisher.

Jason C. Maxwell

ISBN-13: 978-1463767310
ISBN-10: 1463767315

People Who Have Used
Jason In The Past...

Jason Maxwell is an Internet marketing wizard! I've worked with him on several occasions and his knowledge blows me away! He's my go to guy! I'm especially impressed with his expertise in taking offline businesses online. Jason is incredibly clever at online marketing. I always recommend his Local Business Marketing Machine course to all of my students. It's off the charts! Jason Maxwell is the real deal.

Celene Harrelson, The Happypreneur
http://thehappypreneur.com

Jason is a very hard worker and has far exceeded my expectations every time I have done business with him (and my expectations are high!). His innovation and in sight has allowed me to take action on the most important tasks, and with that I have been able to see measurable results in a short period of time. I love that he is so easy to get in touch with and so quick to get me the information I need to keep moving forward. Jason not only has great ideas, but he takes action on them and supports you to develop that habit for yourself in your own business. He has helped me make ideas happen in my business and I have all the faith in the world that he can do the same for you!

Helen Raptoplous
http://FreeProductivityTraining.com/

People Who Have Used
Jason In The Past...(continued)

I've been building my business online for the past 3 years and have run across the good, the bad and the ugly when it comes to solid advice and training. Jason Maxwell is one of the very few I can count on to always be the Good!

Jason has a talent for breaking down what some would consider complex internet marketing concepts into easy to understand, bit-sized action steps that anyone at any level can understand and implement. He has an obvious curiosity for the internet marketing world and is constantly learning and delivering new, effective business strategies.

I'm honored to have been introduced to Jason's work as it has helped me implement great strategies into my business.

Cheers
Tom Buford
TomBufordMarketing.com

Local Business *INSANE* RESULTS

Disclaimer and Copyright Notification:

Copyright © 2011 by **Jason C. Maxwell**
http://JayMaxMarketing.com

The contents are based on the author's personal experience and research. Your results may vary, and will be based on your individual situation and motivation. There are no guarantees concerning the level of success you may experience. Each individual's success depends on his or her background, dedication, desire and motivation.

NOTE: Some of the recommendations in this report might contain affiliate links. If you click on the link(s) and purchase such a product based on my review and/or recommendation, I will receive a referral commission. Whether I receive a commission or not will not have any effect on the purchase price of the product. Additionally I am sometimes offered a complimentary product to review. My decision to promote these products is based on my own satisfaction with the products. I do not recommend crap, and any review I make will be based on my own experiences, which are not typical. You could do better, you could do worse, you could do nothing at all, and that is totally out of my control.

We make every effort to ensure that we accurately represent our products and services. There is no guarantee that your results will match examples published in this report.

Some links may change or even not work for many reasons beyond the control of the author and distributors. They cannot guarantee or otherwise be responsible for what you might find when you click through to sites not under the control of the publisher of this report.

About Jason...

Jason C. Maxwell began his Internet career many years ago as a consultant for several Fortune 500 companies. His career was very successful until the dot-com bust in the early 2000's. This was a paradigm shift for him because he knew that he never again wanted to work for someone else and depend on them for a paycheck.

He struggled for many years to make ends meet until finally he came across the solution. There were an infinite amount of small businesses that were desperately in need of help when it came to their presence online. Now he was not just talking about becoming another website developer, but more specifically his idea was to create amazing marketing plans that would drive massive amounts of customers in their doors.

Around this time Jason also created a call in show that he does every single week online called Ask Jason Maxwell. http://AskJasonMaxwell.com On this show callers are on the line with Jason and they ask him questions about how to market their businesses online.

Jason's online marketing expertise and ability to teach these skills have spawned several best-selling courses in which he teaches people around the world how to help small businesses to get massive amounts of customers coming through their doors.

Jason is also well known online for his ability to create Facebook pages that go viral and get 1,000's of likes within the first day. Combining all these skills and giving you all the secrets is what this book is really about.

Foreword

When I first met Jason several years ago, it was during the depths of the recession that had begun in 2007. It had taken both of us by surprise, and you could see in his eyes that unmistakable despair that grips us like the cold bony hand of a faceless stranger on a stormy winter's night. I knew that he was in for a rocky ride as he made every effort to dig in his heels and grasp at the most narrow strands of hope that every good business owner seeks. I also knew that he would find success beyond his wildest dreams, if he was willing to do what most people will not do – persevere in spite of the odds.

Jason is, as they say in the south, smart as a whip. His intuition and thirst for knowledge knows no bounds. As time went on he tried everything I suggested, questioned it and tried it a dozen other ways, and sought out mentors far more experienced and knowledgeable than myself. And when I finally saw him again in the fall of 2010, there stood before me a confidant young man who held the world in the palm of his hand. Of course, I did not tell him this at the time.

Instead, I put Jason to the ultimate test. Could he rise above everything that had happened to him during the past few years, both personal and professional, to land on his feet as a leader in his field on the Internet and beyond? Indeed, he could.

I've watched Jason as he has metamorphosed from a burgeoning small business owner into an online marketer and trainer who can hold his own among men and women who have been doing this for a decade or more. His intuition when it comes to new media technology, list relationship marketing, and local business marketing strategies continues to amaze and enthrall me. I never hesitate to call him when I have a situation that requires a unique perspective and approach.

He's caught the eye of more than a few marketing gurus who now keep a watchful eye on him to see just what strategies he will unveil next.

To say I am proud of Jason would be understating the obvious; this is someone whose ideas you'll want to bookmark as you climb your own ladder of online success. Read every word of this book. Then read it again. The future of your local business may depend on the knowledge, strategies, techniques, and detailed information Jason is so graciously sharing here.

Connie Ragen Green
ConnieGreen.com

Table of Contents

<u>Dedication</u>

I dedicate this book to my Mom and Dad, who taught me to believe that I could do anything if I put my mind in gear and my butt into action. Thank you so much!

This book is also dedicated to my brother that always stuck by me no matter how low I let my head hang. I love you so much for never giving up on me!

And to all my friends in internet marketing…

Hanging on the wall in front of my desk are my goals and the goals of my clients. Keeping these in front of me is the key to my success. I also have this quote hanging on that wall:

"If you will do for a year what others won't do, you can do for the rest of your life what others can't do!"

~Unknown

Why Internet Marketing?

Why Internet Marketing?

Over the last 10 years or so, the Internet has become more and more ingrained in our daily lives. People use the Internet to search for almost everything, including local businesses and other local information.

And with the explosive growth of smartphones like Blackberries and the iPhone, this move to searching for everything online is just going to happen faster. The fact is that more and more people are using their mobile devices to find out about and purchase products from local businesses. Every smart phone is equipped with apps that allow a person to use GPS to find local businesses in every category, get their phone numbers and even directions to their location.

If you're not reaching your customers (and potential customers) in the places they're searching for information, you're going to get left behind by your competition that is.

In this book, we're going to look at some of the things that you need to be aware of when marketing on the web, as well as some of the ways that you can not only reach new customers, but get your existing customers to spend more money with you, and do it more often. What if you had a way to get 100's of your best customers in your door this afternoon spending money with you.

Would it be worth your time to learn this? You bet it would. You see, ten years from now the businesses that are thriving will be the ones who have taken the time to learn Internet marketing. They will be the ones who are dominating on Facebook and dominating the top spots in the Google search results. They will be the ones who are using text messaging and mobile sites to accept orders and draw in new business.

The old ways and old days of doing business are long gone. If you want to be in business through the next decade it is time to learn about how the Internet works and what you can do with it to grow your business. I predict that in just a few more years there will be no more printed newspapers and magazines.

Even today, people with iPads and other mobile devices are reading dynamic versions of articles through their devices in which they are able to comment on and see live video. The printed page is going to be a thing of the past. Along with it will go the printed ad. Advertising online will be the primary means of motivating buyers into your business.

The Move To Online Search

According to Google, 20 percent of all searches are related to location. And comScore reports that Google served up 10.7 billion searches in April, 2011. That means that approximately 2.14 billion searches were related to location - in other words, local search.

These numbers have been increasing every year over the last several years. Compare them to April, 2008 when Google served up 6.5 billion searches, which means roughly 1.3 billion local searches.

The bottom line is that more and more people are using the Internet to search for local information, including businesses like yours.

And one of the advertising mediums that is

being hit the hardest by this move online is Yellow Pages directories. Traditionally, the Yellow Pages have been the "go to" source for local businesses, and, as a result, if your business wasn't listed in the Yellow Pages, you would be missing out on a lot of potential customers.

But with the transition to Internet-based local search, those searchers are becoming less and less likely to use the Yellow Pages. And not only because of the convenience and speed of the Internet - they're also looking for reliable sources for reviews and other information about the companies they're considering, which isn't possible with print advertising.

The Yellow Pages Dilemma

Yellow page providers realize that they need to do something to keep from becoming extinct in a few more years. One of the solutions they've attempted is Internet-based Yellow Page directories.

These directories work much like the printed version. Your ad gets placed in whatever business category is applicable, on the assumption that people will use those directories to find local businesses. But the reality is that those sites have very little traffic - Google, Bing and Yahoo are the places that people turn to when they're looking for local businesses.

This is good for you for several reasons:

1. You have much more flexibility in how you present your business through the search engines than you do with online Yellow Page directories.

2. Your costs will be much less than what you would pay for an ad in the print version of the Yellow Pages, particularly compared to larger ads.

3. With local search marketing, you can update or make changes to your ads as often as you want. Compare that to a print ad that can only be changed annually.

And on top of all those things, the Internet gives you a much larger reach. Yellow Pages directories generally get distributed once a year, and only to households that have landline phones.

According to a study that the Department of Health and Human Services at the National Center for Health Statistics ran from January to June, 2010, approximately 24.9% of all adults live in households with only wireless phones. They have given up landlines completely.

That means nearly 25% of your target market may not even receive a Yellow Pages directory. They rely on the Internet for virtually 100% of their searches.

And, interestingly, even more children (29%) live in households with no landline phone. So as those children become adults and move out on their own, these numbers are expected to grow.

If you don't believe me then do a poll yourself, today. Ask every person that you see under 30 when was the last time that they picked up a Yellow Pages book to find a business or a service. You will be shocked to hear that many of them are not even aware that there was ever a "book" for this type of activity. Now, while you have their attention, ask them, "If you don't use the yellow pages for information when looking for a product or service what do you use?" About 85% of them are going to look at you and without hesitation say, "Google". Test this out and you will see...

Two more facts that you might find interesting:

1. Half of 18-34 year-old Americans check Facebook the moment they wake up in the morning.

2. That same set of Americans gets the majority of their news from Facebook.

In the next decade, these people will be the primary spenders in our economy. They will be the ones coming in your business and buying things, purchasing services, spending their hard earned dollars. *So what are you doing with your business on Google and on Facebook?*

Connecting With Your Customers Using Google

Connecting With Your Customers Using Google

There are a number of ways you can connect with your customers online, and if you want to get the best results you need to take advantage of as many as possible. Because the Internet makes it so easy for people to find the solutions they're looking for, you can't afford to hope they come to you - you need to meet them wherever they might be searching.

The most important place you need to establish a presence is in the search engines - specifically Google, Yahoo and Bing. Of the three, Google gets the largest percentage of searches (roughly 65% in April 2011, according to comScore) so it is the first place you should focus your efforts. When people talk about searching on the Internet, they even use the newly coined verb "Googling" to represent this action. Google is the undisputed search king.

After you spend time with Google, you need to spend an equal amount of time and effort over at Facebook. Now this goes way beyond just creating a personal profile for yourself. In fact, I am really not talking about a profile page at all. You are in business and Facebook has business pages made specifically for you that will help you to showcase your products and services in a way that will help you to spread across the community socially.

What does that mean, to spread "socially"? Well, you could think of it exponentially, if you like... Basically, it just means that my friends tell their friends and their friends tell their friends.

It spreads like a virus and that is why sometimes it is referred to as viral marketing. We will talk more about this later when I show you how to create a Facebook business page that will get the attention of all of your potential customers in a way that no other can!

When it attracts that kind, of attention it will be likely to spread across your town and community like wild fire, drawing you in lots of business, but like I said...we will discuss this later!

Let's start, though with what you can do with Google to have a presence there and make an impact on your business. There are several aspects to having a presence in Google:

- The search results
- Google Places
- Sponsored ads
- Google Images
- Google News
- Google Video

These are all part of Google, but in many ways they are independent of each other. We're going to cover them all in detail in this book, but it's important to remember that each of them works separately from the others, so you want to show up in as many as possible when your customers are searching for you. If you show up in most or all of them, it's going to create a strong impression with your customers, and make them much more likely to choose you over another business.

And keep in mind that the other search engines have many of these same features. We're going to talk about Google in most parts of this book because they are the largest, but virtually everything we cover translates over to

Bing and Yahoo as well.

When it comes to the most important aspect of Google for a small business there are many ways that you could look at that question. I think that Google ads (called Adwords) can be very effective. Google images, news and video are all important. Yet there is really nothing more important to a small, local business than Google Places. When the average person does a search the Google Places results will be the ones they call first.

So let's take a minute to dissect the anatomy of a Google search result. What are you really seeing? Here is the breakdown for you, simple and easy to understand...

Local Business *INSANE* RESULTS

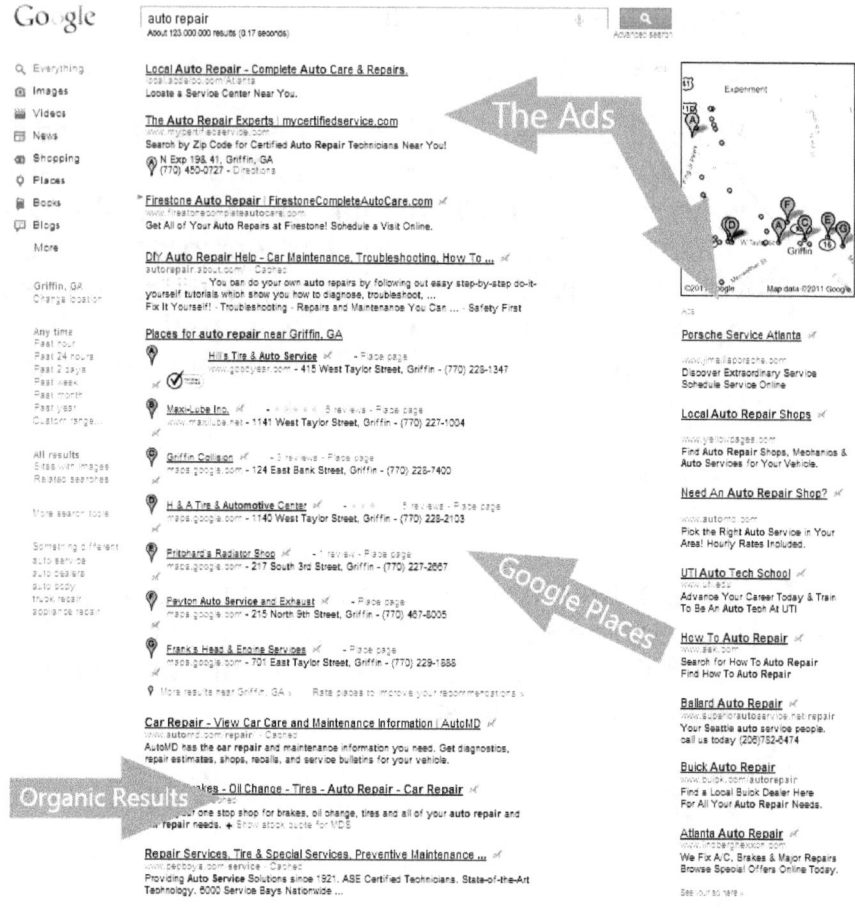

The Anatomy of Google's Results

When you run a search on Google you are actually getting a variety of things in the page that is returned to you. Let me try to break it down so that you understand.

By design, the first thing you see when you run a Google search is ads that are directly related to the keywords you searched for. Typically, there will be two to three ads at the very top of the page and up to seven ads on the right sidebar of the page. These ads are served up to you thanks to a system called "Google Adwords". This is the primary way that Google creates revenue. (They make about $86.1 million dollars PER DAY, Not too shabby!)

The next thing that you will see when you are running a search for something that Google perceives to be a "local search" is the Google Places results. These are the important ones, more on this later.

Finally you will see what are known as the organic search results. The websites that are found by Google's search engine and are ranked according to how relevant they are to the words you have searched for. Many things go into this ranking system and there are two things that we know about it.

1. No one totally understands how it works...except maybe the CEO of Google.

2. It's always changing and evolving, so when you do figure it out...it changes!

In other parts of this book we will talk about Google Ads and how to get ranked highly in the organic results. For now we will talk about the part of the results that are most important to small businesses.

Google Places

Google has a service for local businesses called Google Places. This service lets you set up a profile for your business where you can showcase various things, such as:

- Special promotions
- Offers
- Photos and videos

Google Places also lets your customers post reviews about your business and you can respond to those reviews, creating a dialog with those people.

Your Google Places listing will show up when someone searches for the products or services you offer in your area, along with other companies offering the same things.

Now imagine how this process is going to work for a moment. When someone goes online to search for a company that provides the solutions you can, they're going to see several results in Google Places. What is going to make them choose one over another?

One aspect will be the ranking in Google Places. The top 3 results get the majority of their attention, with the first one getting more than the rest. So you want to be sure your listing is at or near the top of those results. (We'll look at some strategies for accomplishing this shortly.)

Another aspect is how much information is shared. If your company has a full profile with pictures, reviews, special offers and other information, it's a lot more likely to get the searcher's attention than another listing that just has the bare minimum information showing.

If this is a potential customer's first impression of your business, you need to be sure you're putting your best foot forward.

So let me show you how to get listed on Google Places...

Getting Listed Highly On Google Places...

Step One: Visit http://places.google.com and click the link labeled "Get Your Business Found On Google" (You will need to sign into Google)

Step Two: The first thing you will do is enter your business phone number. Google will try to locate your business with this number.

Step Three: Next you will enter your information about your business. This is a very important step in making sure you are in the top of the Google Places results.

1. Make sure you title your business with keywords (i.e. Smith Realty would be "Real Estate Broker – Smith Realty"

2. Make sure the description uses the same keyword phrase (i.e. "We are the local choice for *YourTown's real estate* needs. We specialize in *real estate services*, we are a full service *real estate brokerage*.")

Local Business **INSANE** RESULTS

3. Include your website (your website address should have your keywords in it, i.e. http://YourTownRealEstate.com) more on choosing an address for your website later.

4. Choose an appropriate category (you can choose up to five)

5. Choose your service area, select a distance radius that you are willing to choose.

6. Add photos of your business, your products, or your customers.

7. Add a video from YouTube. If you do not have any videos on YouTube you can create a cool, fun little video that looks very professional at http://jaymaxmarketing.com/animoto all you need is photos/videos and they do the rest...for free (30 second videos are free)

After you click submit Google Places will send you a postcard to your business address to verify that you are the legitimate business owner. Once you get the postcard (usually within a week) they will give you a code to put into the Places.Google.com site.

Once you do that, the Places listing will be up. Once it is up, you need to get some reviews up on your places account. The best way to do this is to offer great customer service.

You can also ask your customers to sign into their Google accounts in your business and write a review for you. When you have a customer who is very happy about what you have done for them that is a great time to ask them to do this as a favor for you. Most of them will gladly do it and you really only need about three to five great reviews to stand out from all your competition.

People who love or **HATE** your service will tell others about it online. Sometimes this can be good and other times this can be really bad. Customer reviews are very often used by the people who search for you on Google to determine which company they are going to do business with. In most industries at the time of this writing your competition will have no reviews or only one or two reviews.

Let me tell you how bad a bad review can be for you...

I had a customer one time that had a rental business. A customer felt they had had a bad experience and so they went onto Google Places and gave her a scathing review. ***Bad reviews on Google Places always show up ahead of good reviews.***

So no matter how many of her other customers gave her a good review the bad one always showed up first.

It took about six months, and us talking to the disgruntled customer to get the review removed.

Search Engine Optimization

Search Engine Optimization

A lot of the things we've discussed in this book come under a subject known as search engine optimization, or SEO. This is the process of optimizing your site to improve your rankings in the search engines. Some of this involves things you can do on your site, such as using the "keywords" that your potential customers are using to find your site within the content of your pages.

There are tools that will help you determine exactly what those keywords are, such as the Google Keyword Tool. This tool is designed for Google Adwords advertisers, to help them figure out what keywords to bid on for their ads. But it works just as well for figuring out exactly what people are searching for. Because the things that people actually search for might not be what you would expect.

Let's look at a quick example. This screenshot shows a search for "bellingham plumbers" (Bellingham is a city in Washington with a population of about 80,000 and 200,000 in the metro area).

Keyword ideas (59)			
Keyword	Competition	Global Monthly Searches	Local Monthly Searches
bellingham plumber		720	590
plumbers in seattle		1,600	1,600
bellingham plumbers		880	720
plumbers bellingham		880	720
plumber bellingham		720	590
plumber		1,000,000	450,000
plumbers		673,000	368,000
plumbing bellingham		590	480
plumbers in bellingham wa		73	73
plumbing contractors		33,100	27,100
bellingham plumbing		590	480
plumbing questions		4,400	2,900
plumbing repair		27,100	22,200
plumber seattle		2,400	2,400
plumber in bellingham		320	260
plumbing problems		12,100	8,100
plumbing services		49,500	22,200
bellingham map		3,600	2,900
pex plumbing		12,100	12,100
emergency plumbing		18,100	8,100

This is just a few of the keywords that the tool returns, but you can see what people are searching for and roughly how many times each keyword gets searched every month.

You can see the keyword phrase "bellingham plumber" (the one we searched for here) gets 590 local monthly searches. That's 590 potential customers who are searching for that term every month, on average.

"Plumbers in seattle" isn't directly related, since Seattle is about a two hour drive from Bellingham. But because it's relatively close, Google still shows it in the results.

You can see several other variations on the main keyword we searched for:

- Bellingham plumbers
- Plumber bellingham
- Plumbers bellingham
- Plumbers in bellingham wa

If you owned a plumbing business in Bellingham, you would want to work these variations into the content on your website to help improve your SEO and get ranked higher in the results when people are searching for those terms.

More SEO

The other part of Search Engine Optimization involves things you post on other sites, like press releases, videos, images and various other types of content. The links that point back to your website from these places will help your site's ranking improve.

And the more sites that have links pointing back to your site, the better. Part of the calculation that Google and other search engines use to rank your website is the number of links, and the "power" of the websites they're on.

For example, if you had a link pointing to your website from a site like CNN.com it would be considerably more valuable to your ranking than a link from BobsWebsite.com.

There are various ways you can generate these links to your website. We've already discussed some of them, when we looked at media distribution. Articles, videos and various other types of media can include links to your website, so as you distribute them to more and more places you will generate more and more links back to your site.

You can also buy links on other websites. This is essentially a form of advertising, but instead of paying for another site to display your banner or paying for clicks on Google or Facebook, you're paying another site to link back to yours with the goal being better rankings.

Getting involved with some of sites we've already discussed elsewhere in this report can also help generate more links to your site. If you're active on Facebook and Twitter, you can use those sites to link to your website. Review sites like Yelp.com will also have links back to your website.

You can even set up multiple websites of your own, each with a very narrow focus. All of them can link back to your main site, helping to push its rankings up. For example, you might set up "minisites" for different product lines that you sell, or different services that you offer – each with a very specific focus. And these sites won't just be useful for linking back to your main website, they can also generate even more visitors and new customers as people find them in the search engines and various other places.

As you can see, many of these strategies work in tandem with one another. Media distribution doesn't just get your name out there, it helps with SEO. Being active on Facebook and Twitter doesn't just give your customers another way to contact you, it also helps your website rank better.

The more you market your business online, the more everything will compound to give you better and better results.

But keep in mind that SEO is not a one-time thing. You can ease back on the amount of content that you are distributing to various places once you've made an initial push to get your site ranked, but to maintain those rankings you'll need to do a certain amount of this on an ongoing basis. Otherwise, if your competitors are also improving their SEO, they could knock your site down and replace it in the rankings.

Tracking Your Results

Something that is fairly unique to the Internet, compared to many other advertising methods, is how much information you can track about where your customers are coming from and which sources are the most (and least) profitable for you.

The nature of the Internet lets you track the source of every visitor to your website so you can tell how many potential customers are arriving from Google, Facebook, videos on

YouTube and any other place you post your content.

You can even track these sources down to specific messages or media. For example, if you post a video on YouTube, you can code a special tracking link into it so you know exactly how many people end up visiting your website as a result of that specific video.

If you do any other advertising, like flyer or Yellow Pages, do you know how many visitors those sources are sending you? Probably not - there's really no way to track them with any accuracy, beyond asking every customer where they heard about you.

There are many tracking services available to you, ranging from free solutions to hundreds, or even thousands of dollars per month. One of the most effective is actually free to use – Google Analytics.

Google Analytics will track visitors coming to your website, where they're coming from and many other things. It will even tell you what keywords people searched for when they found your website in the search results.

This data can be invaluable to you because over time you can analyze it and work it back into your website to get even better results.

For example, using our Bellingham plumber example again, when you analyze your site's data you might find that you're getting traffic from Google for the phrase "bellingham plumbing and heating" – a phrase you didn't do any optimization for.

Seeing that, you could hop over to Google and see just where your site ranks for that term. Let's say you find it towards the bottom of the page, maybe spot 7 or 8 (there are normally ten results shown on each page).

From this research, you now know two important things – people are already finding your site using that phrase and you could quite likely improve your ranking by doing a little bit of SEO for that phrase.

You might write a new article to add to your website that uses the phrase "bellingham plumbing and heating" or you might just add it to a page or two that are already on the site.

Simply by doing this little bit of work, you would most likely start getting more visitors who are searching for that term because your site would move higher in the rankings.

Google Analytics doesn't just track your visitors, however – it can also track the actions those visitors take once they arrive at your website.

For example, if you have a lead capture form on your site to get people's name and email address so you can follow up with them in the future, you can track the people who actually sign up for your email list. With Google Analytics, you could track all the way from the click on one of your ads through to someone signing up to receive your emails.

And from there, you could use tracking codes to identify those people when they come into your place of business or contact you for more information. This lets you track the exact cost per customer by calculating your advertising cost versus the number of people who wind up doing business with you.

You'll know which advertising sources are most profitable, which ones are not working very well at all, and which ones are generating the most new leads. This is the type of detail that is extremely difficult, if not impossible to track through traditional advertising mediums like Yellow Page and newspaper ads.

Creating Your Website

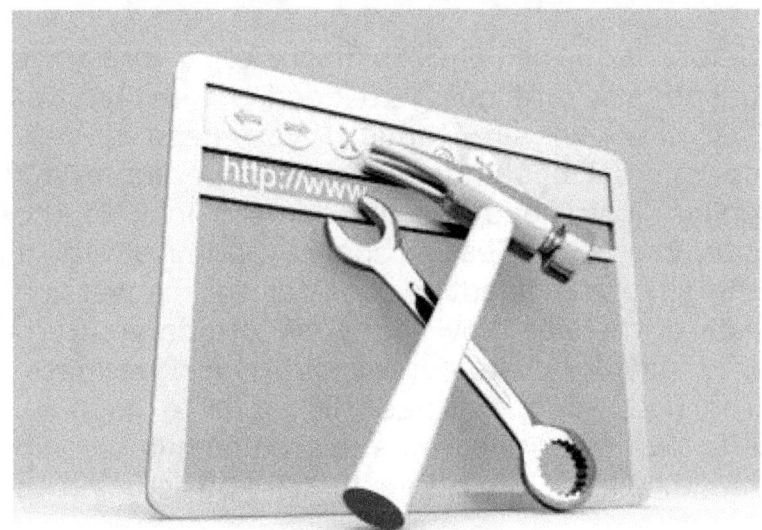

Creating Your Website – Getting Started

Before you can have much of a presence online, you are going to need a website. Not just any old site though, you need a very specific set of things in order to be successful online. You need to consider the look of the site, the SEO (Search engine Optimization) of the site, you need to consider the conversion rate of the site...how many visitors do you turn into paying customers inside your business. The first thing you need in order to have an effective website is to have an effective domain name. What I am about to tell you is going to shock you.

Creating Your Website – Domain Names

So let's talk about an effective way to set up the SEO (Search Engine Optimization) for this business. The very first thing that you are going to need is a good domain name. Now many business get really confused when it comes to getting a great website name.

Now if you were that Bellingham plumber we were talking about earlier then it might make sense to you to have a website name that honored the name of your family business. Let's say your company is called Smith Plumbing Co. So you go out to Godaddy.com and you search and you are happy when you find that SmithPlumbingCompany.com is available. So you spend the $11.99 and you register the domain.

You have just made your first mistake in setting up your website!

You see when it comes to setting up your website so that it can be found by the search engines you have just violated the first rule of SEO.

#1 Rule: Websites are ranked primarily based on the keywords that are found in their main URL (web name or address)

Now that you know the first rule of SEO, let me ask you a question. How many people are going to the search engines and typing in "Smith Plumbing Company"?

Well the truth of the matter is that hardly ANYONE is doing that. The people that are doing that obviously already know about your business, and they most likely would already be considered customers of yours. So by purchasing that domain name you didn't help yourself. Instead of choosing a domain like that, why not go back to the Google Keyword Tool and work off of those suggestions. Take a look at the keywords that are getting traffic and then try to find website URLs that are exact matches.

So take a look at the list again...

Keyword ideas (59)

Keyword	Competition	Global Monthly Searches	Local Monthly Searches
bellingham plumber		720	590
plumbers in seattle		1,600	1,600
bellingham plumbers		880	720
plumbers bellingham		880	720
plumber bellingham		720	590
plumber		1,000,000	450,000
plumbers		673,000	368,000
plumbing bellingham		590	480
plumbers in bellingham wa		73	73
plumbing contractors		33,100	27,100
bellingham plumbing		590	480
plumbing questions		4,400	2,900
plumbing repair		27,100	22,200
plumber seattle		2,400	2,400
plumber in bellingham		320	260
plumbing problems		12,100	8,100
plumbing services		49,500	22,200
bellingham map		3,600	2,900
pex plumbing		12,100	12,100
emergency plumbing		18,100	8,100

One thing I do want to point out before we go much further is the columns. The first column is the actual keyword. This is pretty self explanatory. The next is the competition.

What they are ranking here is the competition for that keyword phrase on their Adwords system. (Remember, Adwords is the Google ads system that allows them to place ads at the top and on the side of the Google search engine results).

So a high amount of competion would just mean that you would have to pay more for ads, if you chose to run ads. That has nothing to do with SEO though and so it should basically be ignored.

The next column is the global monthly searches and it means exactly what it says. How many searches were run in the last month for that particular keyword phrase. To be more specific what they are showing you is the average month, over the last 12 months. So for instance if you have had 1200 searches in a year, this column would show 100. Even if the majority of the hits had happened in December or in July.

The next column is a place that many of my customers get tricked. It says local searches and so they assume that it means how many times was this keyword searched in their local area. That would be incorrect. Actually what they are talking about here is how many searches occurred in the USA (or whichever country you are in at the time that you run this report).

The good news is, unless there are a lot of cities named "Bellingham" then it is highly likely that most of these searches are being run out of your area.

Your next step is to go over to GoDaddy and find out if there is a domain available for that particular keyword phrase. You can go directly to GoDaddy.com but if you do you will pay $11.99 for the domains. Instead if you go through this link here you will get a special discount that I have arranged with GoDaddy for the readers of this book.

http://jaymaxmarketing.com/godaddy

NOTE: *In order to get this special deal make sure that you are not signed in. It will tell you that they are going to charge you $11.99 all the way till the end of the process. Then at the very end you will see the price change to $7.67*

Here is where you need to go to get that deal http://jaymaxmarketing.com/godaddy

One other thing worth mentioning is that when you are buying your domain at Godaddy they are very good at upselling you all kinds of things that you really do not need. When you are going through the buying process DO NOT BUY ANYTHING BUT THE DOMAIN...you do not need any of their extra services.

So back to SEO now...when you go to GoDaddy and you find the domain that you want (the one that has the keyword phrase in it), buy it. Typically it is better to go ahead and buy it for 5 years instead of one. The search engines can tell the difference and you are seen as more of a legitimate business if you have purchased a domain for long term rather than for just a year or so.

So let's say that you bought the domain name http://BellinghamPlumbers.com

When you implement the ideas that I am going to tell you about later in this book you are going to shoot right to the top of the search engine results and be seen by at least those 590 people who are running that search. If you just got in an extra 100 calls every month that would be huge wouldn't it?

Creating Your Website – Hosting/WP

The next thing that you need to be concerned with is hosting. Which host you choose really has a lot to do with your website being found because of what things they have in place for you to use. I recommend to all my clients that you choose a host which offers CPanel Hosting. There are several choices in the market place for this type of hosting, but I prefer BlueHost.

http://jaymaxmarketing.com/bluehost

The reason you want CPanel hosting is so that you can do most of the webmaster work yourself without needing to hire a webmaster. Most all of the SEO experts today will tell you that you need to build your website on something called Wordpress. Well, what is Wordpress?

Wordpress is typically thought of as a blogging platform, but it is really so much more than that. Wordpress is actually an Operating System. Wordpress allows you to do so many things, and the way it is designed you will get the most SEO for your buck.

Wordpress can look any way that you want it to look. Most people think of Wordpress looking like a blog. Here is my local business blog...

While this is a popular use for Wordpress, remember that I said before that Wordpress is an operating system. You can make it look however you please. This site here was created with Worpdress as well...

Wordpress is not only able to look however you want, it has loads of hidden functionality that you can use to make your website work better and be seen by the search engines and ranked higher. One of the greatest things about Worpdress is that it is "open-source". That means that the code is available to everyone and people can develop new solutions that tie into the main Wordpress functionality.

These solutions are called "plugins". At present count there are over 15,287 plugins available for free at Wordpress.org. There are thousands of other plugins available for sale all over the Internet. If you can think of something that you would like your website to do then there is likely a plugin that will do it for you...automatically.

Wordpress allows a person with just an average amount of skill to make and maintain great looking websites with ease. One caveat though...

There are two versions of Wordpress out there. There is Wordpress.com and Wordpress.org. Now that may seem like pretty much the same thing, and if you go to those two sites it will appear as if they are really close to being the same thing. They are not the same thing at all. Wordpress.com is a version of WP that allows you to host your stuff, for free with them. You end up with an address that looks like this http://YouSiteName.Wordpress.com.

Now while this may sound like a cost effective way for a business to get a presence online, this is NOT the way you want to go. Everyone I trusted told me this when I first got started, but I still made the mistake and did it. I spent weeks working on it and it turned out to be a total waste of time. ***Please do not make the same mistake that I made.***

When you are ready to get serious about business the version of WP that you want to use is Wordpress.org. If you choose Bluehost as your hosting provider you actually don't have to download anything. Everything is already done for you inside the CPanel. All you have to do is make a few clicks and you will have a fresh install of Wordpress on your new domain.

I have created a 10 minute video that shows you step by step how to install Wordpress on your CPanel hosting account. Go to this site to see that quick, free video

http://jaymaxmarketing.com/installwordpress

Creating Your Website – Plugins

As you will remember earlier we talked a little bit about plugins for your WP site. Plugin allow you to do more things than an entire book could explain to you, much less one small section in a chapter. That being said I will give you the basics of plugins.

Plugins add additional functionality to your website. For instance, let's say that you wanted to have a Contact Us form on your website. Well you could hire a programmer to design one for you or you could use a simple free plugin. Which sounds easier to you? Here are the steps to creating a contact us page on your site.

The first step is to download and install the plugin. From the Dashboard go over to the section on the left labeled Plugins and click add new. In the field that appears type in this:

"WP-Simple-Contact-Form-with-Captcha"

(no quotes)

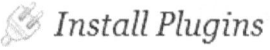

Install Plugins

Search | Upload | Featured | Popular | Newest | Recently Updated

Plugins extend and expand the functionality of WordPress. You may automatic

Search

Search for plugins by keyword, author, or tag.

Term | ▼ | WP-Simple-Contact-Form | (Search Plugins)

Then click search plugins. There will now be a list on your screen of results. Click "install now" on the first one which is called WP-Simple-Contact-Form-with-Captcha. Accept the questions it asks you and activate the plugin.

Now under settings on the left hand side you will see a link labeled "Simple Contact Form Options" click on that link. You will enter the email address that you want your contact us form to send emails to. You will enter the subject line of the emails (so that you will recognize them in your inbox).

You will enter the number of characters you want in the capcha code. (this is the annoying little code on webforms that you have to look at and type in the letters/numbers, to prove that you are a real human and not a bot). I normally choose four; you may choose how many ever you want.

Now you will want to copy the little short code that is on this page because we are about to use it.

Simple Contact Form options

Send completed form to	Jason@JayMaxMarketing.com
Subject heading of mail	Potential client
Number of letters in capcha	4

Submit

Usage

To use WP Simple Contact Form, simply add a page with the following text: [wp_simple_contact_form]

Your next step is to create a page and call it "Contact Us". You would do this from within the Dashboard of Wordpress. Once you are in there look over on the left side for the link under Pages that is labeled "Add New". Click that link and a new page appears. Title the page "Contact Us"

In the area where you would normally write text just paste in the short code you copied earlier. The code is: [wp_simple_contact_form]

Once this code is in place click the "Update" button and then view your page

Name	John Customer
Email	John@Bellsouth.net
Subject	More info

Message

I would like more information about your products and services. I saw your website and it looks like you have some great deals. Please contact me at my email address or call me at (404) 555-1234

John

ynidy

Enter the text above   ynidy

Submit

Effective SEO – Plugins (cont'd)

Now you have a great looking contact us form and it cost you nothing except about five minutes of your time to set up. Now you can see the power of the Wordpress system and the power specifically of plugins.

Here are some plugins that you should consider when you are building your site for your business:

- ✓ Wordpress SEO – Tool to help you get the most SEO from a page or a post

- ✓ WP-Twin (Allows you to back-up your entire site in two clicks and replicate it anywhere) Special bonus at this link to change non-Wordpress sites into Wordpress. http://JayMaxMarketing.com/wptwin

- ✓ Category Icons – Allows you to have icons for each category named the same as your keywords to increase SEO

- ✓ Dagon Design Sitemap Generator Plus – builds a regular sitemap to increase SEO

- ✓ Efficient Related Posts - Adds posts at the bottom of your posts that are similar to keep people on your site.

- ✓ Google Sitemap Generator - builds an XML sitemap for your site

- ✓ Google Analytics by Yoast - Allows you to connect your site to Google Analytics to track your hits and traffic

- ✓ SEO Image – Attaches keywords to images to boost SEO rankings and scores.

- ✓ SEO slugs – Shortens the permalinks to the best keywords

- ✓ Sphere related content - gets you more traffic by placing your posts and pages on a network

- ✓ Stumble For Wordpress - gets you more traffic by placing your posts and pages on a network

- ✓ TinyMCE Advanced – Gives you added functionality to your posts and pages (makes it more like using MS Word)

- ✓ Twitter Tools – Allows you to tie in your twitter account to your blog so that your posts will be tweeted and your tweets will show up in the sidebar.

- ✓ WP DB Optimizer – Needs to be run about once a month to make sure the database inside WP is operating efficiently

- ✓ WP Sticky – Allows you to make a post stick to the top of the posts and not get moved down.

- ✓ WP Super Cache – Allows your site to load faster, which is one of the things search engines are looking at for SEO

Creating Your Website – Ping Lists

When you create your site and add pages and posts you want to make sure that it gets picked up by all the major search engines. One of the best ways to do this is to ping them to let them know what you have just posted. When you ping a server you are basically sending them a little message to let them know you have done something that they need to check out.

This is a common practice in Internet marketing and not only is it totally kosher it is something that the search engines want you to do so that they can have the most up to date information available to their users.

In order to set up your pinging go to your Dashboard inside WP and click on Writing under the tab labeled Settings on the left hand side. Now go to the bottom of the page where you will find a section labeled "Update Services". This is where you are going to cut and paste in the ping list.

A ping list is basically a list of servers on the web that accept pings from blogs and websites. These ping servers let all the search engines and other relevant news sites know that you have posted new and interesting information so that they search engines can come take a look at your site and make sure that everything is indexed correctly.

Ping lists are something that are added to and taken away quite often so instead of giving you a list of ping servers in this book I will just give you a website address that I maintain for keeping this list. All my clients, students, and even I go to this site when I am ready to cut and paste in the ping list.

http://jaymaxmarketing.com/pinglist

Go to this site and cut and paste the list into the "Update Services" section of your dashboard and don't forget to click the "save Changes" button before you navigate away from that page.

Creating Your Website – Themes

Once your WP site is installed and you have added the right plugins then you will need to choose a theme for your site. A theme is basically a skin that causes the site to look one way or another.

Think of it like this. You could go out today and buy an iPhone and install lots of apps, all your contacts, and lots of photos and videos. If two weeks from now you decided to get a pink cover for your phone it would totally change the look of your phone, but it wouldn't change any of the content inside your phone.

This is exactly how a theme works. You are able to change the look and feel of a site without changing the information contained within the site. There are 1,411 free themes available today for Wordpress within the Wordpress.org website. There are 1,000s more that you can get from just going to Google and typing in "Free Wordpress Themes". There are also paid themes that you can get.

For the most part I always recommend people downloading the free themes for their website. At least at first, remember you can always change this later and you are trying to get the best SEO and traffic you can at this point. In that game it is the words that matter, not the look and feel. In fact, I say this all the time...the Internet runs on words like cars run on gasoline.

When you have downloaded your theme, go to your Wordpress dashboard and I will show you how easy it is to activate it. When you get to the dashboard go to the area on the left labeled "Appearance", and click on the link labeled "Themes"

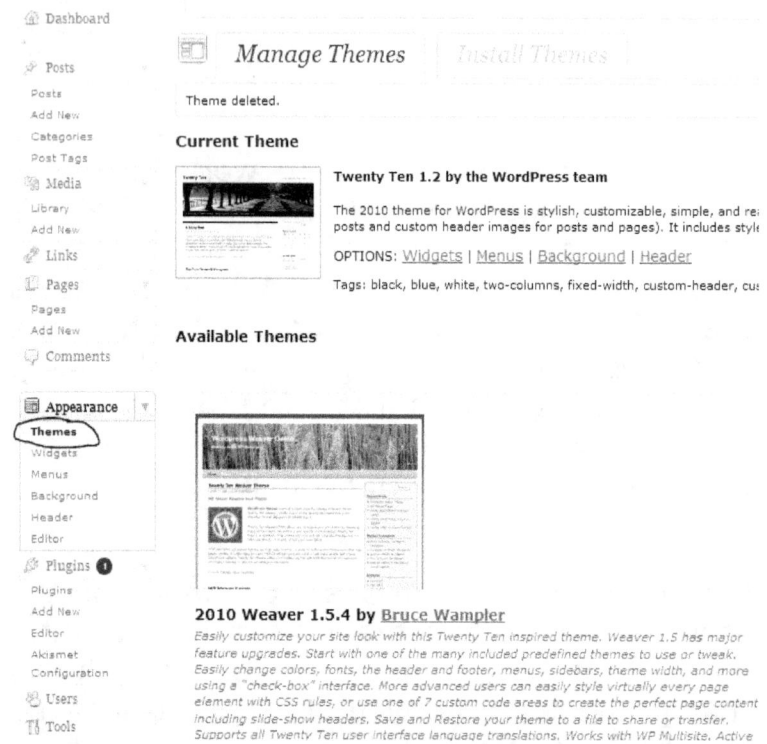

Once you are there click on the tab at the top labeled "Install Themes" and then click on upload. (If you have not found a theme online and you want to search for one, here is the place to do it.) For the purposes of this exercise I am going to assume that you have downloaded a theme off the Internet. Themes will come to you in .zip format.

Do not unzip them. Upload them to your WP in that .zip format.

Local Business *MSANE* RESULTS

After you click "install now" it will install the theme and then ask you to activate it. Once you have done so it will change the entire look and feel of your site. Here is what the site looked like before we activated the theme:

Eating Healthy While On A Budget

Posted on by admin

Register Domain Name www.Register.com
Domains from a Trusted & Reliable Award Winning Service. Order Today!

Get $75 Free Advertising www.Google.com/AdWords
Promote Your Business On Google. Claim Your $75 Coupon Now!

$6.99 Domain Names www.Network-Solutions.com
Special Offer: Domains Only $6.99. By the Original Domain Registrar!

1200 Calorie Diet www.ediets.com/diet-plans
Is A 1200 Calorie Diet Plan Right For You? Find Out More Here.

AdChoices ▷

Just about everyone wants to eat better, but being on a tight budget sometimes makes healthy eating a difficult goal. It's important however, to buy the healthiest food you can afford, whether you are cooking for yourself or for a growing family. Using coupons is another great way to make a food budget stretch. Cutting coupons is a great way to save money on products you already

Tell Google You think this site is cool...
+1 0

Recent Posts
- Eating Healthy While On A Budget
- Recipes for Chinese Food Fried Rice
- Cooking Healthy and With Less Fat
- How to Choose Register or Transfer a Domain
- Eating healthy and staying fit with the perfect recipes

And just seconds later, after I activated that new theme...

You can see how themes can make a real difference in how your site appears to your customers.

There is no doubt that Wordpress is the way to go when it comes to building a website for your small business. There are too many positives and rarely a negative.

From search engine optimization to ease of use, to the multitude of plugins and themes that you can choose from Wordpress is the way to go.

Creating Your Website - Permalinks

The last thing I want to talk to you about is permalinks. What are permalinks?

Permalinks are links or URLs that point to a specific blog post or page on a website. These links remain unchanged indefinitely so they are less susceptible to what is known as "link rot" (when links expire or are dead it is referred to as "link rot")

The default inside Wordpress is for the permalink to be the number of the posting. A typical permalink looks something like this:

```
http://YourKeywordPhrase.com/?p=123
```

This works fine for websites. When you send someone to this link they will get the information they are looking for.

Local Business *INSANE* RESULTS

The problem is, this **SUCKS** for search engine optimization. Remember the first rule of search engine optimization:

> *Websites are ranked primarily based on the keywords that are found in their main URL (web name or address)*

Well the second part of this is that the next biggest ranking factor for search engines is what appears before or after the main URL. So in the case of the site above using the permalink:

?p=123

How much good do you think that does you in the eyes of the search engines? *That's right, you are learning, it doesn't do you ANY good at all.*

So how do you fix this problem with the permalinks? Well, it is actually pretty easy. Go to your WP Dashboard and under the tab on the left labeled Settings click on the link labeled "Permalinks".

You should now see the settings for your permalinks. I want you to click on the selector for "Custom Structure" and type in the following:

/%postname%/

After you do that click the "Save Changes" button

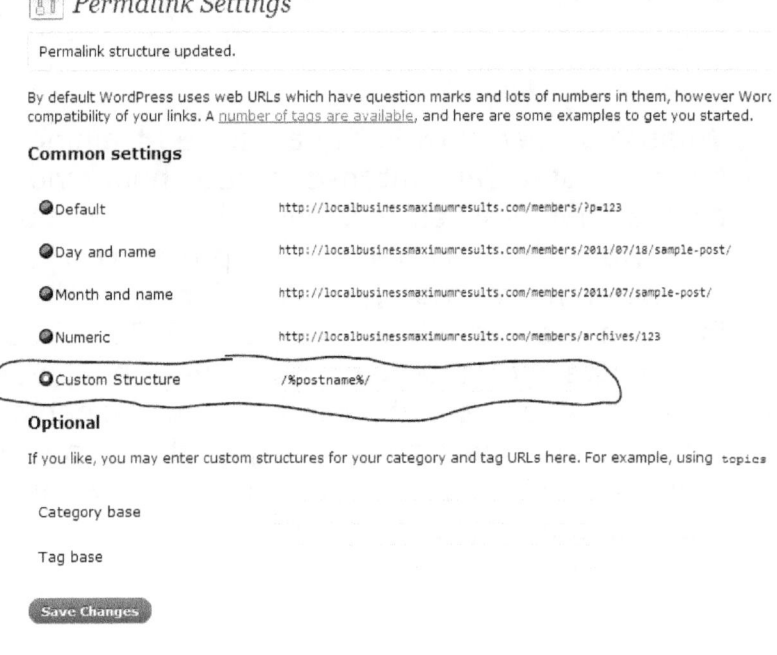

Local Business *INSANE* RESULTS

Now when you go back and take a look at your posts and pages you will see the permalink has changed to become the keyword rich post/page title.

http://YourKeywordPhrase.com/more-good-keywords

Creating Your Website – Advanced Training

What I have done here is give you a basic overview of what you need to do to get your site off the ground and started so that the search engines will rank it and make you get traffic.

What you need now is the advanced training. I have created an intense three hour video course that teaches you everything you could ever want to know about Wordpress. Yet, it is so much more than just Wordpress. I have included a module called "FIRE Your Webmaster" that teaches you everything you need to know about creating and managing websites. The best part is I teach this in a way that you will be able to do it all without knowing any HTML or nerd stuff.

The program is called "How To Become A Webmaster". Here is a little bit about it:

How To Become A Webmaster shows people how to get tremendous results with their WordPress blog.

This series of video lessons breaks down the art of quickly tweaking your blog for maximum performance. These tweaks will help you get better rankings in the search engines, more traffic and ultimately more sales.

Plus you get the bonus training that will teach you all the technical stuff for being your own webmaster. I teach it in a way that even a non-techie can get it and break free from expensive webmasters and their fees.

Get started with this link to the training:
http://HowToBecomeAWebmaster.com

Brand Marketing

Brand Marketing

One of the biggest hurdles for a lot of business owners to leap when it comes to the Internet is realizing that people will be talking about your company whether you like it or not.

And that includes good AND bad. Mistakes are bound to happen in any business, but when they do, it's quite possible that the story will wind up on the Internet where anyone searching for your business can find it.

If you're not maintaining an effective presence on the web, you're going to have two problems if this happens.

1. The negative review could wind up ranking high in the search results, so whenever somebody searches for your business, this could be one of the first things they see. The review might be accurate if a mistake really was made, or it might be completely inaccurate, but that potential customer has no way of knowing for sure (and is more than likely going to accept it as fact).

2. You won't have a chance to explain the situation and fix it.

The solution here is to be a part of the conversation. In other words, engage your customers where these kinds of things might appear so you can try to correct any mistakes that were actually made, or explain your side if it's completely inaccurate.

We've already discussed two of the places that these kinds of discussions can happen - Facebook and Twitter. It's important that you have a presence on both, if only as a point of contact for your customers who are already in those places.

Imagine this scenario...

One of your employees has been dealing with a customer, and the customer is unhappy with the service they received. But instead of coming to you and giving you the opportunity to fix the problem, they go to these websites and post about the problem and how unhappy they were with your company.

If you don't have a presence on Twitter or Facebook, you might never know about it. But people who are looking for information about your company online could quite likely find that information whenever they search for you.

Now think about this...

If you are active on those sites, on the other hand, you can jump in and try to correct the situation. This is not only going to give you a chance to turn an unhappy customer into a happy one (who might also become one of your biggest supporters at that point) it's also going to add your side of things to the "record" of the situation on the Internet.

Now when someone searching for you finds that review/complaint, they're also going to see your response, and the fact that you tried to correct the situation for that unhappy customer.

Which scenario would you prefer?

Review Sites

Another place that it's important to maintain an active presence is review sites, including:

- Yelp.com
- Where.com
- Citysearch.com
- Insiderpages.com
- Yahoo Local
- Google Maps

These sites are local business directories of a sort, which let people post ratings about reviews about them. Much like any other website we've discussed, you need to maintain a presence here if you want to be able to manage your brand and what people are saying about it.

One of the reasons these sites are so important is many of them have apps for the iPhone and other smartphones, so a lot of people use them to look up local businesses when they're on the go. If they find a listing with low ratings or bad reviews, they can just choose another one - the business owner will never know they lost a potential customer.

Just like Facebook and Twitter, you want to have an opportunity to either correct the problem or explain your side of it when these low ratings and review happen.

These sites aren't only about reviews, however. Many of them let you make special offers to your customers, in the way of discounts, giveaways and more. These special offers can be another great way to draw in both new and existing customers through their smartphones and other mobile devices.

If they are searching for a local business using one of these services, seeing an offer from your company will make them a lot more likely to visit. And if it's combined with good reviews and interaction on your part, it's going to cement their decision even more firmly.

Social Media Sites

One of the fastest growing segments of the Internet over the last few years is what's known as Social Media. Facebook and Twitter are the two most well-known examples of social media sites.

Having a Facebook page is becoming more and more important, because people have come to expect it. There are over 600 million users on Facebook, and if you don't have a presence there you're missing out on a lot of potential business.

Plus, for many people Facebook has become synonymous with the Internet. A lot of people spend most of their time online using Facebook, so if you aren't reaching them there, you may not have a chance to reach them at all.

Facebook started out as a way to connect on a personal level, but over the last couple of years they have added a lot of features that are targeted at businesses. You've probably already started to notice a lot of big companies adding "Find us on Facebook" to their websites, advertising and other places.

It can work just as well for local businesses; in fact it can work even better. Because Facebook is by nature a place to be "social" a local business fits in much better than a big, faceless corporation.

Setting up a Facebook Page for your business gives you a way to connect with your customers "virtually" and it can help to create a real sense of community.

Twitter is another social media site where you should definitely have a presence. It's a little different beast, because the whole point is to post short updates (up to 140 characters at a time) so you can only share so much information.

It can be useful for sending out messages about special offers and other news, but more importantly it's another way for your customers and potential customers to contact you.

Your customers can send you messages, called "Tweets", via Twitter so it is similar to email in some ways. But because the messages are so short, it can be an effective way for them to ask quick questions or give you quick feedback, without having to invest a lot of time to do it.

Aside from reaching potential customers, there's another reason you should have a presence in these places - managing your brand. People will talk about their experiences with your company on the Internet whether you're part of it or not. It's important that you are.

Engaging Customers

Another aspect of managing your brand online is simply engaging your customers. This comes back to have a Facebook Page, setting up a Twitter account for your business and all the other things we've talked about.

This lets you connect with your customers without any of the cost associated with traditional advertising.

Local Business *InSANE* RESULTS

For example, if you have a Facebook Page where your customers can follow you, you can offer special promotions and other offers through it. A lot of people spend a great deal of their online time using Facebook, so you can reach a lot of people this way, with no advertising costs at all.

Let's look at a pub as an example. It's a Wednesday afternoon and the week has been slower than normal. They've got an order arriving on Friday but still have too much inventory of a particular brand of beer from the previous one. They've been building a following on Facebook by letting their customers know about their page. So they post a special offer on Facebook for that brand of beer, good for the next two days.

Do you think that might bring in a few customers who wouldn't have otherwise showed up over the next couple of days? Probably, and they more than likely won't stop with the special promotion, they'll order food as well. So a free promotion could turn a losing situation into additional profit for that business.

Creating A Facebook Business Page

Why Does Facebook Even Matter?

People tell me all the time that they want to do business online, but they don't understand why Facebook matters. Well, it does it matters in a huge way. Here are some statistics that I feel prove my point in an amazing way:

Facebook is taking over the world...

a. Over 600 million active users and well on their way to getting over 1 billion
b. 50% of those people log on, on any given day
c. People spend over 700 billion minutes on Facebook every month
d. 48% of 18-34 year olds check Facebook when they wake up
e. Average user is connected to 80 pages, events, and groups
f. 71% of Internet users in the USA have their own Facebook profile.
g. Over 250 million people access Facebook thru their mobile device.
h. Facebook login and Facebook.com were the number one and number two most searched terms for the last two years.
i. 48% of young Americans said they find out about news through Facebook
j. On this past new year's eve, a record breaking 750 million photos were uploaded to Facebook

In just 20 minutes on Facebook:

1 million links area shared, 2 million friend requests are accepted and almost 3 million messages are sent, 1.5 million event invites are sent, 2.7 million photos uploaded, 1.3 million photos are tagged, 1.5 million wall posts, 10 million comments made.

Facebook is something serious!

So as a business owner how does all this translate to you? Maybe you have a personal profile, maybe you have even created a Facebook business page. So far though you have not seen any bags of money dropping from the heavens or huge amounts of customers begging to get into your business to pay you money.

Let me ask you a question...did you watch the Super bowl last year? If you did, you know that the commercials were very special. Well, the commercials for the Super bowl are always quite popular, but this past year they all had one thing in common. All these huge companies that spent millions of dollars to be advertised during the biggest event of the year all shared one unique thing in their ads.

In every one of these very expensive ads there was not a single mention of the company's corporate website. Instead, at the end of each ad all the advertisers were calling the viewers to do one thing...visit them on Facebook.

WOW...can I say that again? WOW!!!

Why would advertisers spend millions of dollars to promote someone else's website?

They would do it because they know that sending them to their Facebook business page is far better than sending them to their own website, why?

When you visit a company's website, you spend a little bit of time there and then you leave. Unless they spend advertising dollars again, they are unlikely to see or hear from you again.

When they send you to their Facebook business page, things are much different. You see when a person "Likes" a business page that business now has the ability to show that customer special offers anytime they want.

When a person has "Liked" your page every time you post a new status, that status appears on that person's wall. That means not only do they see it, but all of their friends see it. Guess what happens when you as a business post an interesting status? The friends of the people that originally "liked" you see it and now they "like" you too.

Guess what happens next...their friends see it...their friends "like" it and it goes on and on and on. This is called viral marketing and there is no better way to do this than by using Facebook.

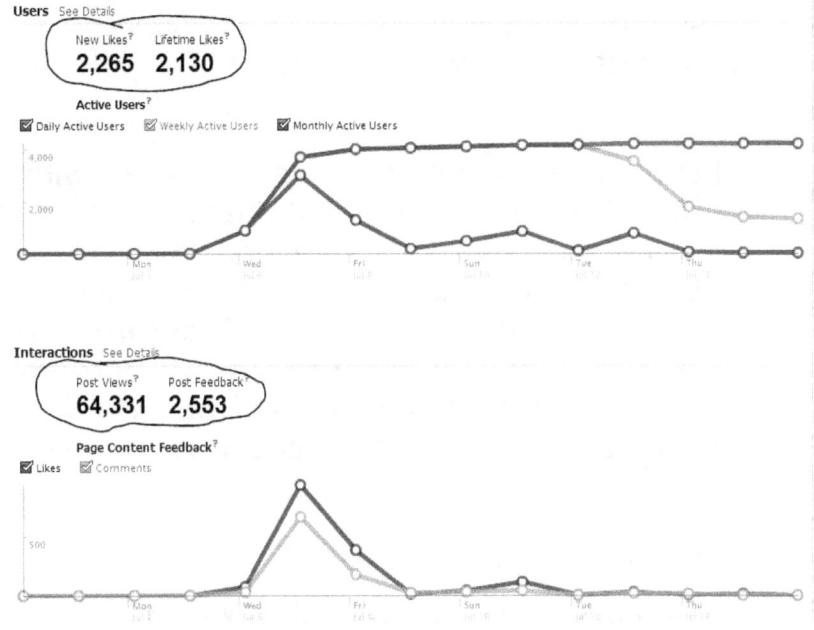

That is how I was able to get a Facebook page to grow from one to over two thousand in less than 24 hours. It begins to spread so fast that you really cannot stop it.

This is the activity on that Facebook page for a ten day period...64,331 views. Would you like that many people to see your offer?

Do you want to take this a step further? Later in this book I am going to talk to you about email marketing. Email marketing is one of the most effective forms of marketing in the world. Imagine having an email list of all your customers that you can send out specials and other offers to anytime you want?

There is a secret way to do this within Facebook as well. It is called the Facebook App (application). While it is beyond the scope of this book to describe how to create a Facebook App I will tell you this. **With a Facebook App you are able to capture the full name, primary email address, and all the likes and interests of your potential customer.**

Think about that for a minute...

Think about how powerful that would be to be able to gather all that information about a potential customer and to have an automated way of marketing your products and services to them so that they are excited to get your emails and spend lots of money with you.

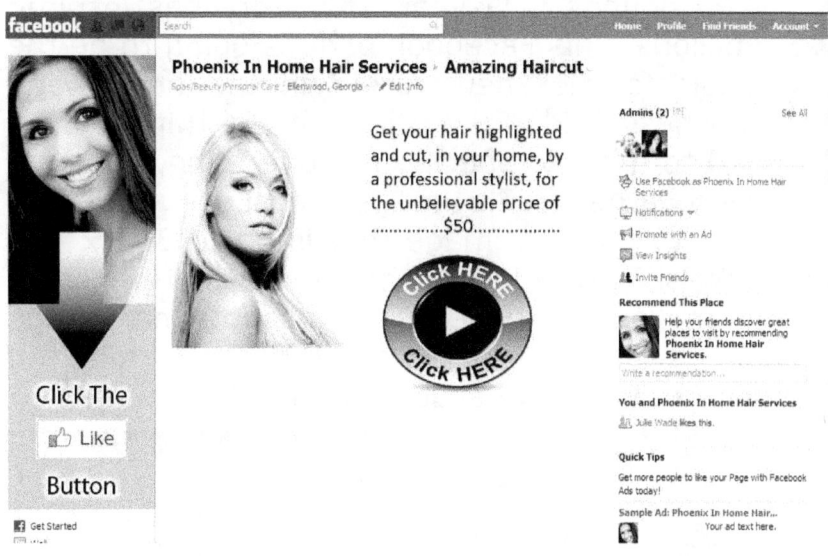

If you are interested in a Facebook App for your businesses, contact me with the information at the end of this book and I will give you a free consultation that will help you to decide if an App is the right marketing tool for your business.

Here is an example of a Facebook page I created for one of the stars of **Extreme Makeover Weight Loss Edition.** Rachel Oliver is an amazing person who lost just at 200 pounds in a year. Her story has inspired millions. This Facebook page is going to be the basis for her new career in the health and wellness field. Take a look at the things that I did to make it special. For one thing, I used a very large profile image. Facebook will allow you to post an image that is up to 540 x 180 pixels. Take a look at how much more exciting it makes her page. Since posting that image she has seen an increase in the number of people who take action and "like" her page.

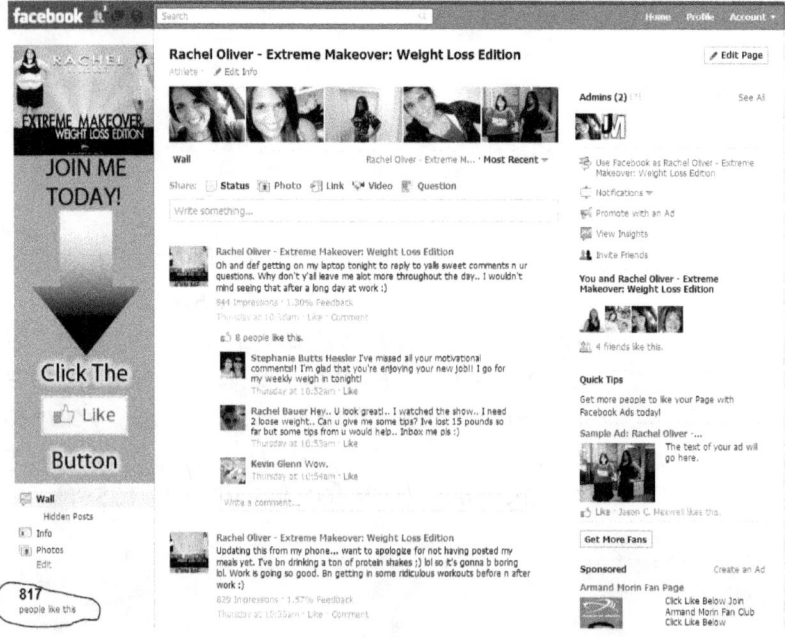

Let's Create A Facebook Business Page

Facebook business pages are basically an extension of your personal profile. So in order to have one you are going to need a personal profile. Most people already have one of these, if you do not it will take you about 5 minutes to sign up for one. All you need is a valid address and you need to be over the age of 13. Once you have your personal profile I want you to go to the bottom of the Facebook page and click on the link labeled "Create A Page"

Click on Create A Page

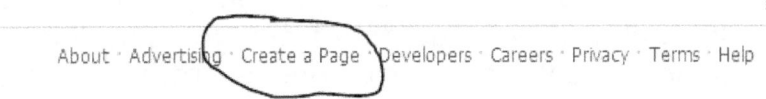

About · Advertising · Create a Page · Developers · Careers · Privacy · Terms · Help

Now you will see a screen that allows you to choose what type of page that you want to build.

Create a Page
Connect with your fans on Facebook.

Local Business or Place

Company, Organization, or Institution

Brand or Product

Artist, Band or Public Figure

Entertainment

Cause or Community

Choose "Local Business Or Place." When you do that you are going to be given a list of business categories to choose from. Choose the one that best suits your business. Then go ahead and fill out the name of your business and all of the address and other details they are asking for.

After you fill in that information and click to create your page, you have done all the hard work. The page is up that fast. You will now need to go through and add information about your business, post photos and videos.

When you get 100 likes you will be able to choose a vanity name. So instead of your page having a long ugly URL you will have a URL that looks more like a regular website like this: http://Facebook.com/YourBusinessName.

This is the basic way to create a Facebook business page. Once your page is live, go to other pages that are in your community and "like" them so that you can post on their wall and talk to them about your offers. Contact the owners of these pages and ask them to talk about your business page in their status updates. Post to the page regularly and talk about things that are of interest to your potential customers.

Facebook business pages are indexed by Google, that means that your keywords that you are typing into your Facebook page can show up in the Google search results and can be found by people who are searching for information about your topic in your local area.

Facebook also has an amazing system of ads that you can run for your business page. I will discuss those more in the end of this book, but there are great training courses available also, see the resource list at the end of this book.

To see a really cool example business page that I created to show off some of my skills visit:

http://jaymaxmarketing.com/fanpageexample

You will see there I am using Facebook like a normal website. I have created a menu which has several different options. I have the ability to play videos and have a list of special offers. This is a very slick way to really grab the attention of people with your business page. If you are interested in learning more about custom Facebook business pages contact me using the information at the end of this book.

Mobile Marketing

Mobile Marketing

Mobile marketing is a huge growth opportunity for local businesses. More and more people are carrying smartphones that have always-on Internet connections, and they're using them to find local businesses when they're on the go.

There are very few businesses that approach mobile marketing correctly, however.

Most companies have either no "mobile" version of their website, or if they do it's really just a smaller version of the same site. The latter is a little better option, but it's still not very effective.

As far as the first problem - having no mobile-specific version of your website - this makes it extremely likely that someone searching for more information will simply leave the page and look for another site that's friendlier.

Look at this website for the City of Boston, for example:

This is what a "regular" website looks like on a typical smartphone. It's practically impossible to read, and even if someone zooms in to see what's there, it's still not going to be very effective.

Having a mobile-friendly version of your website is a better option. You can see what the City of Boston's mobile site looks like in this example:

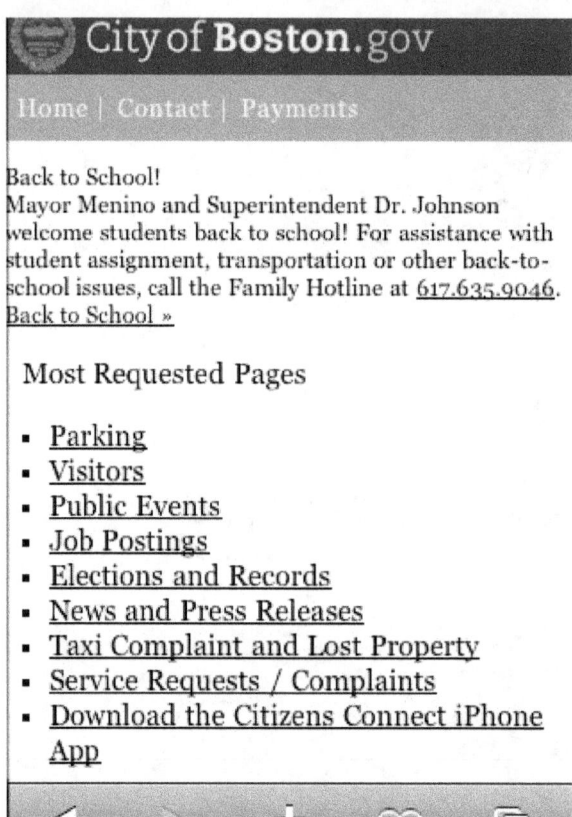

Much easier to read, right?

This type of site might be fine for the City of Boston, since people are more than likely looking for information. But it isn't the best option for local businesses. After all, what are people looking for when they look up a business on their mobile phone?

99% of the time, they're looking for one of two things - a phone number or an address. They don't want to read the website or anything else, they're just trying to either call or get to the right location.

Let's look at an example of a much more effective mobile website:

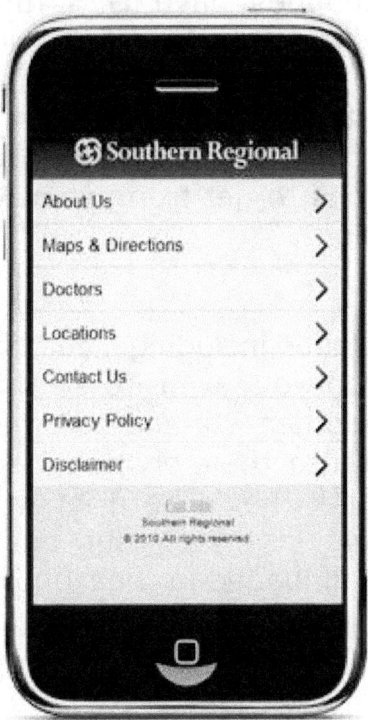

If someone searches for a local business on their smartphone, and winds up on a page like this, don't you think the chances are much better that they're going to actually call and/or visit as a result?

And that's not all you can do with mobile websites. Most of today's smartphones have various other functions that can be integrated into a mobile site.

Many smartphones have GPS functions built right in. What if you could include GPS coordinates on your website so all your potential customer had to do was click on the link and it would open their GPS and give them exact directions to get from wherever they are to your location?

Or how about including all that contact information on your website so that customer could click another link and automatically have it all loaded into their phone's address book? Don't you think they'd be a lot more likely to make multiple visits to your business if the details were all loaded in their phone whenever they needed your products or services?

But there's one more incredibly powerful aspect of mobile marketing that is still extremely under-used by local businesses - text messaging.

Text Messaging

Text messaging, or SMS, has experienced huge growth in the number of people who use it regularly. And it's not only younger people who are using it - it's becoming more and more common with older users as well.

Local businesses can use text messaging to engage their customers on a much more personal basis than even email marketing can provide.

There are two huge advantages to text messaging that really can't be matched by any other method of communication.

1. Most people have their phones with them virtually all the time, so those messages will reach them no matter where they are.

2. The vast majority of text messages get read almost instantly when they're received. Compare that to email that may go unopened for several days.

How can this work in your favor? Going back to our pub example, text messaging could work much the same as Facebook promotions, except it would be even more immediate.

If the pub was slow on a particular day, they could send a text message at 5:00pm and reasonably expect a response that same evening. There's just no other advertising medium that can reach your customers as immediately that is virtually guaranteed to be seen.

So does that mean you need to be feverishly tapping out text messages to all your customers every time you want to send something?

Not at all. There are services that will broadcast a text message to everyone who has requested to receive them from you. These services let you choose a number, called a Short Code, to use as your point of contact.

Your customers just have to send a text to that number to sign up to receive text messages from you whenever you broadcast something out.

You can even set up an automatic response from these short codes, giving you the ability to offer an incentive to get people to opt into receiving those messages.

For example, a restaurant might offer a coupon for a free appetizer on their next visit by texting the word "appie" to their short code number. When the customer sends the text, they get a response virtually instantly with the details of how to get the free appetizer. This can be as simple as "Show this message to your server on your next visit to claim your free appetizer." But now whenever you broadcast a text message, they will receive it virtually instantly.

Coupon Sites

"Deal of the day" sites like Groupon and Living Social are another highly effective way to reach people through their mobile devices. You can advertise a special offer on these sites, which have apps for smartphones like the iPhone and Blackberry.

These apps offer what is known as "push" notifications of new specials. This works very similar to a text message – when a new offer is posted, the app displays a message on the phone.

Let's look at Groupon.com as an example, since it's the largest of these sites.

You list a special offer of some type with Groupon, offering a discounted price, a two-for-one special or any number of other special deals. Groupon posts the deal on their website, sends it out by email and pushes it to all the users of their mobile applications.

Because the offers are geographical, only people in your general area will see it by default. The users of the service benefit by getting a great deal on what you sell and your company benefits by getting a bunch of new customers who might never heard of you otherwise.

Plus, people outside of your immediate market can also view your offer, and buy it as a gift for someone who lives nearby. So you can reach people who don't even use the service via the people that do.

Keys To An
Effective Website

Keys To An Effective Website

Having a good mobile version is one aspect of an effective website, but there are several things that your main website should offer as well. Your website is responsible for several things:

- Educating your audience
- Branding your company
- Establishing your expertise in your industry
- Generating leads and sales
- Building relationships with your audience

There are also a couple of things it's NOT responsible for, however:

- Miraculously drawing in people searching for what you offer
- Replacing personal connection and interaction

One mistake that a lot of companies make is trying to cram as much information as possible into the home page of their site. This is a sure-fire way to overwhelm any new visitors, and in many cases they will just click away and keep looking.

Instead, use the home page to grab the visitor's attention and help them find the right page on the site for whatever information they're looking for. Think of it as a sort of "directory" for the rest of the site. You want people to be able to find what they want within 5 seconds of landing on your website if at all possible.

Try to look at your website from the perspective of someone who doesn't know your company and may not even know what you offer. If you look at it from the perspective of someone who already knows everything there is to know about your business, it makes it much harder to optimize for your visitors.

If you find it hard to distance yourself from your business this way, an effective way to do it is to create a customer "avatar" that you can use as a model for your typical customer.

Create a fictional customer who has most of the traits of your typical client. Give them a name, consider their age, their sex, what kind of knowledge they have about your product, their income, how many kids they have, etc. The more complete this avatar is, the better.

Then, whenever you are writing something for your customers, whether your website, an email, an article or any number of other types of content, write it as though you're addressing that fictional customer directly. This can really help to filter out the stuff that's either unnecessary or confusing and get right to the point you want to make.

We'll talk about how to get the people who are searching for what you offer to actually visit your website shortly (in fact, that's really the ultimate goal of everything in this book) but as far as personal connection and interaction goes, the Internet has one very useful tool for this - email.

One of the most critical things you should be doing on your website is some kind of lead capture - getting your customers' names and email addresses so you can contact them via email.

Email Marketing

"66% of those surveyed said they had made a purchase because of a marketing message received through email."

- ExactTarget, "2008 Channel Preference Survey"

Every page on your website should have an opt-in form where people can sign up to receive your emails. While text messages, Facebook and various other methods of contacting customers are important, email is still one of the most widely used technologies on the Internet.

Virtually everybody has an email address, and by building a list of your customers' names and email addresses, you can keep in touch with them on a regular basis to keep your company at the top of their mind.

You can send various things via email:

- Upcoming promotions
- Coupons
- Newsletter
- How-to information
- Anything else that would be relevant to your customers

Unlike flyers or other types of advertising, email doesn't have a per-message cost. Whether you send 20 emails a month or 2,000 emails a month, your cost isn't going to change by much, if at all.

What that means for you is that you can send an email as often as you like, and you can do it on short notice. So if you have a special event coming up or some other special promotion that you want to remind your customers about, it's just a matter of writing a quick email and sending it out to them a couple of days ahead of the event.

But it's not just a tool for sending special promotions like this. You can also use what's called an "autoresponder" to automate a certain amount of your email contact.

When a customer signs up to receive your emails, an autoresponder service will automatically send a certain number of messages at whatever interval you want. This lets you queue up a number of emails that will go out to your customers with absolutely no effort on your part.

You can use these emails to educate your customers about the products or services you offer, educate them about how to use those same products or services, or even just send monthly reminders that you are there to help if they need it.

You could even use it to send reminders of appointments or other due dates. For example, a dentist's office could send a reminder via email a day or two ahead of a scheduled appointment (not to mention a text message with the same information the day of the appointment) or a car dealer could send a reminder that it's time for the next oil change at the proper time following a customer's last visit.

And perhaps best of all, email is a two-way communication tool so you can even use it to ask your customers for feedback. There are various ways to take advantage of this:

- Ask them what their biggest questions are about the products you sell, so you can tailor your advertising and other promotions to answer those questions.

- Ask them what products or services they want or need that you don't currently offer.

- Get feedback and testimonials from them that you can use in future promotions

When you do this, you're not going to get responses from every customer who receives your email. In fact, you may only receive a couple of responses. But the responses you do get could help you make a lot more profit simply by providing the products or services that your customers are actually looking for.

How do you get people to sign up to receive your emails? There are various strategies that will work.

If you deal with people in person in your business, such as a retail shop or restaurant for example, you can have a computer or a portable device such as an iPad where people can enter their name and email address right at the point of sale.

This is considerably more effective than the low-tech method still used by a lot of businesses – a notebook and pen. Why have your customer write their name and email address in a notebook when you can have them enter it directly into a lead-capture form on a computer? This puts them directly into your email service's database so you don't have to manually enter that information yourself.

Plus, if you use a device like an iPad you'll often get even more people who will sign up to receive your emails because they want to "play" with the device a bit. Even if it's just a matter of entering their information on your lead capture form, the novelty is still there.

Another effective way to get people to sign up to receive your emails is on your website itself.

Add a lead capture form (known as an "optin box") to every page on your website so people can enter their name and email address no matter what page they might be looking at.

To increase the number of people who sign up to receive your emails, you can offer them some sort of incentive for doing so. This could be something like a free report or white paper that will help educate them about the products or services you offer, or it could be some sort of special offer or coupon that gets sent to them automatically after they sign up to receive your emails.

Or you could do both to improve your conversions even further. Offering a report or white paper has another advantage as well – you can use it to promote all the reasons why a potential customer would want to deal with your business as opposed to your competition.

That's not to say you need to badmouth your competitors. Just explain why your company is their best choice, and what unique benefits you can offer. If you provide them with a report that helps them learn more about what you have to offer them, and then include a bit of a sales pitch at the end, it can generate a lot of new customers for your company.

You can also use what is known as an "exit popup" on your website. This is a popup window that gets displayed when someone goes to leave your website. This popup can make essentially the same offer as the optin forms on every other page of your website, but it has been proven that these popup windows are more effective at convincing visitors to sign up for your email list.

The worst case is they will leave without signing up, but they were leaving your website anyway so why not make one last attempt at capturing their contact information?

Another way to get people to sign up to receive your emails is to use other advertising media to help promote it. If you send out flyers, include a brief call to action on each one letting people know they can sign up to receive special offers and other information by email by visiting your website.

If you want to continue running Yellow Page ads even after reading this book, include that same call to action in your ad the next time you renew and have the opportunity to change it.

You could even add a message to the end of every customer receipt or invoice, asking them to sign up for your emails at your website.

Treat this email list as a valuable part of your business – because it is – and promote it anywhere and everywhere you can.

Multiple Methods Of Contact

Your website should make it easy for your customers to contact you, no matter what method of communication they prefer. All the places they can get in touch with you should be easily found when they arrive at your website. This includes things such as:

- Your phone number
- Your address
- Links to other websites like Facebook and Twitter
- A "contact us" form where they can send you a message directly from the website

The more ways you give your customers to contact you, the more likely it is that they will. And different people prefer different methods, so make it easy for each of them to do it the way they want.

If you're really ambitious, and it fits the way you do business, you could even offer a live chat function on your website that lets your visitors chat with someone directly over the Internet.

This is similar to a telephone conversation in many ways, except the communication is typed through the chat service instead.

This method of contact won't work for every business, but if you or a staff member is sitting in front of the computer for much of the day, it may work for you. And while it may seem a bit "anti-social" to some people, there are a lot of people who aren't comfortable calling and speaking to you "in person" but would be very comfortable chatting over the Internet instead.

Promotional Strategies

Local Business *InSANE* RESULTS

Promotional Strategies

One of the biggest advantages of using the Internet to reach new customers is the low cost of advertising, and the speed at which you can implement, test and change things. There are many different promotional strategies you can use to both improve your rankings in the search engines and get your business listed in various other locations.

Press releases are an effective way to do this, for a couple of reasons. First, when you send out a press release, it is going to get listed on a lot of news websites quite quickly. Because you can include a link back to your site in the press release, it can drive a lot of potential customers directly to your site as well as help improve your site's rankings (which of course will also result in more potential customers).

And second, your press release might actually get noticed by a local newspaper and you could wind up getting some free press out of it. Many local newspapers are desperate for stories about people or businesses in their town. If you have something newsworthy in your press release, this is exactly the type of story they would like to print. And the fact that you're local just makes it that much better, since they can contact you for further information if need be.

There are a number of press release services that will distribute your press release to various newspapers, websites and other media outlets. Some of the most effective include:

- PRWeb.com
- Webwire.com
- Marketwire.com
- PR.com
- PRlog.com
- WirePRNews.com
- PRLeap.com (paid, but really good)

You submit your press release to these services, and they in turn broadcast them out to many different news outlets, both online and offline. The cost of these services varies, depending on the number of outlets they broadcast to and what other additional services they provide.

If you distribute press releases on a regular basis, you will not only be more likely to get noticed by one or more media outlets, you will also get SEO (Search Engine Optimization) benefits that can help your website rank higher in the search engines, and ultimately generate more traffic.

We'll look at SEO in more detail shortly.

Media distribution is another highly effective way to get more customers to your website. This means submitting articles, video, images and other types of content to various sites. When your content get posted on those sites, it can result in new customers coming as a result of both finding that content and your website's ranking improving.

Video Distribution

Video is one of the most powerful types of media you can use. We already mentioned adding images and video to your Google Places page, but that's not the only place those types of content can be used. There are dozens of video sharing sites, the most widely used being YouTube, where you can also share your videos. Some of the other popular video sites include:

- Vimeo.com
- Dailymotion.com
- Veoh.com
- Justin.tv
- Buzznet.com
- Collegehumor.com
- Ustream.tv
- Revver.com

Some sites are focused on certain types of videos, such as Collegehumor.com which is focused on funny videos. Other sites have a wide range of topics, like YouTube.com, so you can post virtually any type of video.

Those videos could be a commercial format, or they could be something more educational if that style suits your business.

For example, if you operate a computer store you could set up a YouTube channel where you show people how to do various things with their computers. This would give you two opportunities to reach your customers.

First, people searching for a local computer store could find your videos on Google or another search engine, and they would see how knowledgeable you were. If you have a collection of videos showing various things they need to know to use a new computer, you'll have set yourself up as the local expert before they ever set foot in your store.

And second, you could use this as a benefit for your existing customers. They could get tutorials about their computer on YouTube, and you could even take questions from them via email, Facebook or various other sources and create videos explaining how to do whatever they're having trouble with.

Do you think that would help cement your customer relationships a little more effectively?

By submitting your video to multiple sites, you will extend your reach to more potential customers. Not only can they find the video on those sites directly, they can discover them through search engines like Google Video. You just never know where people will find your content, so the more places you can share it, the better.

Article Distribution

Article distribution is another highly effective way to reach your customers online. There are just as many article directories as there are video sharing sites, if not more. Some of the most effective sites to get your articles distributed include:

- Ezinearticles.com
- GoArticles.com
- Articlesbase.com
- WebProNews.com
- ArticleDashboard.com
- Article-buzz.com
- Submit Your Article
  http://JayMaxMarketing.com/submityourarticle

While all of these sites area great, I highly recommend that you check out Submit Your Article, for a low price they distribute your articles out to thousands of websites. This is a very cost effective way of distributing your articles without lots of hard work.

Much like video sharing sites, some article distribution sites are more focused on certain topics, such as WebProNews.com which is mainly online marketing related information, while others cover virtually everything.

The way these sites work is you submit your article to get published on their website. You can include a short "bio" at the end of the article, telling the reader what your company offers along with a link back to your website.

The link in your bio has two benefits:

1. People who read the article will click on the link to visit your website, and once they do they can sign up for your email list, read more about your company or anything else that you offer on your site.

2. The link helps your website rank higher in Google and other search engines, so the more articles you distribute, the

better you will rank when people are searching for local businesses.

The real power of these article sites is in the syndication features they offer. Most of these sites let other websites use your article on their site, as long as they leave your bio intact at the end of it. So as other sites syndicate your article, you will get even more opportunities to reach your customers as well as more and more backlinks helping to push your site up in the rankings.

And while all this is happening, you will help to establish your reputation as an expert. If someone goes searching for reviews or more information about your company, they will find all these different websites where your articles are posted. This will help make you the local expert.

After all, if you saw the same author's articles in every magazine you read about a particular topic, you would probably think they know a little something about that subject, wouldn't you?

Being mentioned all over the Internet has the same effect. If you want to really see the power of **Submit Your Articles** go to Google and type in "Jason C. Maxwell" I dominate the first ten pages of search results.

Images

Images are another type of content that can help you extend your reach and get your company in front of potential customers. There are many different photo sharing sites where you can post these pictures:

- Flickr.com
- Photobucket.com
- Imageshack.com
- Imgur.com
- Picasa.com
- Smugmug.com

The value here is twofold. First, if it suits your business, you can share pictures of the products you sell, work you do or almost anything else. For example, an interior designer could share images of past jobs or before and after shots.

For someone searching for a local interior designer, a picture is worth a thousand words, so having those pictures available for people to easily find can be invaluable. Google and most other search engines have mixed images into their search results, so you could end up attracting a potential customer's attention through those images.

But even if your business doesn't necessarily translate well into pictures, there are reasons you might want to distribute images to these sites.

One reason is for brand recognition. If people are searching online for what you offer and your company name or logo comes up in the search results, that will help to brand you in their mind. When they see your website listed in the search results, or find your Google Places listing on their smartphone the next time they go searching, they're going to recognize you over other companies that they haven't heard of.

And if you have pictures of your office or place of business online, it's going to make it easier for them to recognize when they get there.

All these things make dealing with your company a little easier for your customers, and when you add them all up it can make a big difference.

Paid Advertising

There are also a number of places that you can buy advertising on the Internet, including:

- Pay per click (PPC) ads
- Banner ads
- Direct ad buys with other websites
- Facebook ads

Pay per click ads are one of the most cost effective. These are the "sponsored ads" that are displayed at the top and right of the search results on Google, Yahoo and Bing.

The way these ads work is you only pay whenever someone actually clicks on your ad, not when it gets displayed. And the cost per click can range anywhere from a few cents to several dollars, depending on what industry you are in and what keywords you're bidding on.

You create ad campaigns based on keywords that people who would be searching for your business might use to find it.

For example, if you were in the tool rental business you might bid on some of the following keywords:

- <city name> tool rentals
- <city name> power rake rental
- <city name> sump pump rental

...and so on.

You can set it up so your ads will only get displayed to anyone who is actually in your city or general area, which means that even if someone in another part of the country were searching for these phrases, your ads wouldn't be displayed.

Because you can control exactly where your ads get displayed, you can target the people who would be most likely to become potential customers very specifically.

And while the general keyword might have a high cost-per-click, when you are bidding on the local version of it (with the city name included) the cost is generally much lower. This will depend on the size of your city and the number of competitors who are also bidding on those keywords, however.

Banner Advertising

If you've been online for any length of time yourself, you've more than likely seen banner advertising in action. These are the graphic ads that you see on many sites. There are a number of ways to buy this advertising space. You can work with an ad network that handles the placement of your ads for you - choosing relevant websites, controlling what cities they get displayed in, etc. - or you can work directly with other websites to buy ad space on their pages.

You can even team up with other businesses in your local market to "trade" ad space on each other's websites. There are lots of ways to work with people who don't compete with you directly but would still be getting visitors who would be interested in what you have to offer.

For example, let's say you own a plumbing business. You could partner up with local electricians, realtors, contractors and various other businesses to share ad space on each other's website. Someone who is looking for an electrician will quite likely need a plumber at some point, and vice versa. Someone looking for a realtor may be looking for a whole bunch of other businesses because they're moving to the area and aren't familiar with it yet.

This can even be taken a step further by offering "finder's fees" for any referrals that you get as a result of another local business. You can set up a system that will track any new customers who click through from an ad on one of your partner businesses' website and wind up contacting you.

You can then pay the person who referred them a finder's fee. If you set up these types of partnerships with several other complementary businesses, it can work out well for everyone involved without taking anything away from their own bottom line.

Banner advertising can be very effective, but for local business purposes you need to be sure that you are able to control where your ads get displayed. If you're an electrician in Portland, Oregon, there's really no point in having your ad shown to someone who is surfing the web in Sarasota, Florida.

Facebook Ads

Facebook ads have some things in common with pay per click advertising - you only pay when someone actually clicks on one of your ads and you can target very specific people. The difference is instead of your ads being shown based on keywords that people are searching for, they're displayed based on demographics that you choose.

You have a great deal of control over the ads you display, so you can get very specific with who sees your ads. For example, if you own a gym or fitness club, you could create an ad that would target women between the ages of

35 and 50 who live in your city, have a college education and are interested in other health-related topics.

Then you could create a different ad that would target men with all those same demographics. And another one for each group between the ages of 50 and 60, or any other demographics you wanted. Facebook makes it very easy to put your ad in front of the people who are most likely to be interested in what you have to offer them.

And it also makes it easy to create multiple ads that ultimately bring potential customers to the same offer, but each ad can target a very particular group of people.

Whether or not you use Facebook yourself, keep something in mind - Facebook is growing at a much faster rate than other websites, including Google, so it is becoming more and more important that your business has a presence there, both in the way of a Facebook Page and advertising. This chart shows just how much faster Facebook is growing:

Local Business *INSANE* RESULTS

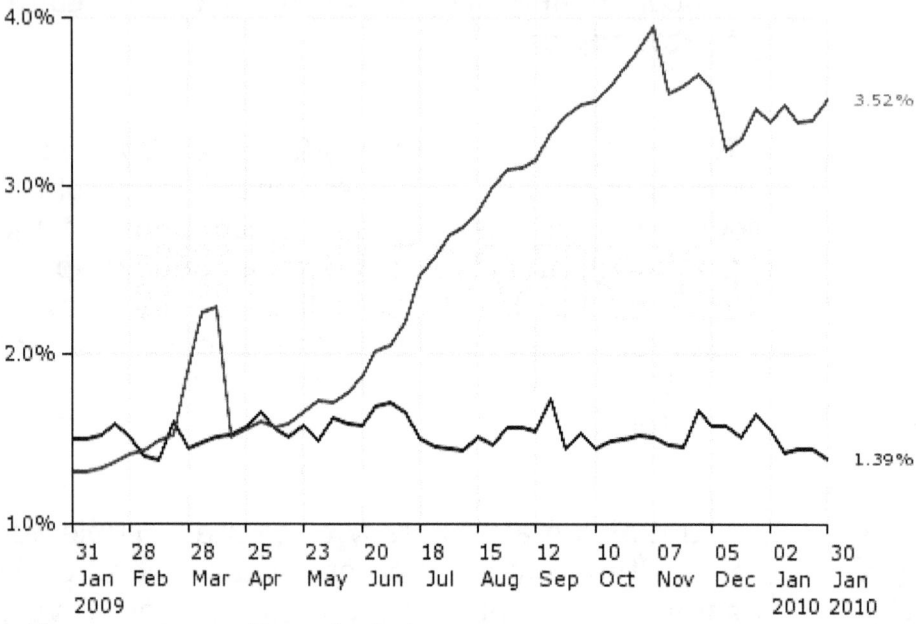

Upstream Visits to News and Media from Google News and Facebook

■ news.google.com ■ www.facebook.com

Weekly upstream % of 'News and Media', based on US usage.
Created: 02/02/2010. © Copyright 1996-2010 Hitwise Pty. Ltd.

An Experian company

The Bottom Line

The bottom line here is that the Internet gives you far better results than most traditional advertising methods. And it's not going anywhere, it's just going to become more and more important to local businesses as time goes on. If you aren't taking advantage of all the opportunities it offers, you have two choices - start taking advantage of them or fall behind when your competition does.

And believe me; your competitors are hearing all these same things. Take a look at this slide, which shows the results of a McKinsey quarterly survey of business executive:

Local Business *INSANE* RESULTS

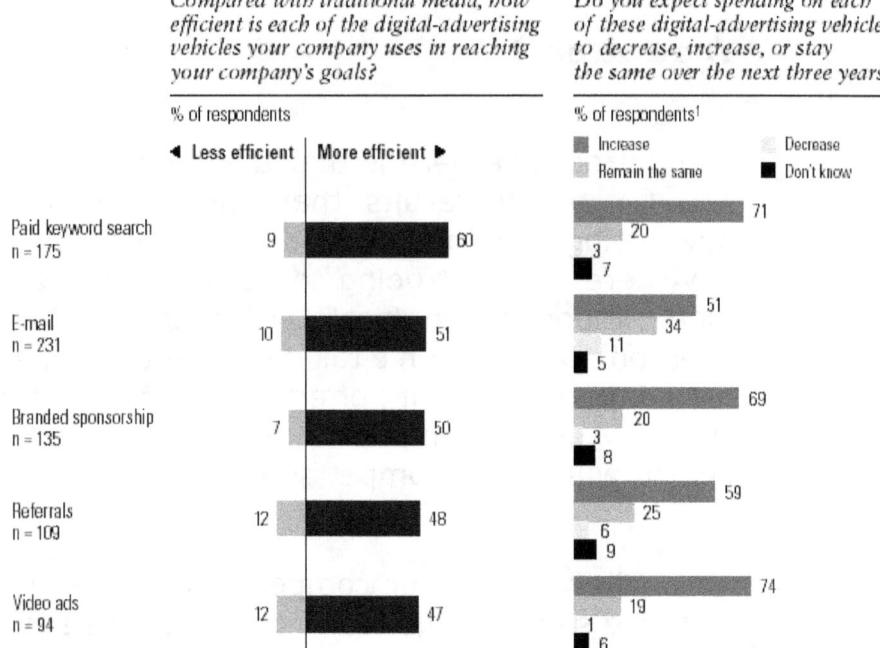

Compared with traditional media, how efficient is each of the digital-advertising vehicles your company uses in reaching your company's goals?

Do you expect spending on each of these digital-advertising vehicles to decrease, increase, or stay the same over the next three years?

% of respondents

◀ Less efficient | More efficient ▶

% of respondents[1]

■ Increase   ■ Decrease
■ Remain the same   ■ Don't know

Vehicle	Less efficient	More efficient	Increase	Remain the same	Decrease	Don't know
Paid keyword search n = 175	9	60	71	20	3	7
E-mail n = 231	10	51	51	34	11	5
Branded sponsorship n = 135	7	50	69	20	3	8
Referrals n = 109	12	48	59	25	6	9
Video ads n = 94	12	47	74	19	1	6

Notice that this survey was done in 2008. These results will be accelerating, not tapering off, as more time passes.

Where Should You Start?

We've covered quite a bit of ground so it's quite likely that you've got a bunch of ideas swimming around in your head, wondering where to start. But let's face it - is this the kind of stuff you want to be doing?

You could probably figure all this technical stuff out for yourself, but is that really the best use of your time? We believe it's important for any business to work on their strengths.

Our company specializes in helping local businesses get more customers by making them findable on the Internet. If you'd like to learn how we can help you find new customers, as well as better engage the ones you already have, all at a much lower cost than most traditional methods of advertising, call us today to set up a free consultation.

Jay Max Marketing

Griffin, GA

http://JayMaxMarketing.com

Jason@JayMaxMarketing.com

As a special thank you for purchasing this book I am including my secret resource list with this book as an additional bonus. These are the tools that I use every single day to profit from the Internet.

Yours truly,

Jason Maxwell

JASON C. MAXWELL'S PRIVATE INTERNET RESOURCE LIST

~For Your Eyes Only~

Table Of Contents

Stuff From Jason

Article Distribution

SubmitYourArticle – Is a tool that has caused me to go from being relatively unknown to dominating the search results for the first ten pages when you search out my name. Give it a try right now and you will see what I mean. Go to Google and type in "Jason C. Maxwell". SYA takes the articles that you write for a client and sends them out to a network of over 1000 other article directories and blogs. This will save you a lot of time. http://jaymaxmarketing.com/submityourarticle

Auto Responders

AWeber – For small businesses who are looking to create a list of customers that they can email to there is no better choice than Aweber. The first month is $1 and each additional month is $19.95. This site will help you create simple web forms that collect the name and email address of the people who visit your client's sites. It also allows you to create a sequence of emails that go out automatically to the customers to tell them about specials, educate them about the client's business, introduce them to the team, http://jaymaxmarketing.com/aweber

GetResponse - If you don't know GetResponse, it's one of the largest, email marketing services for small businesses, like you and me. Their new Form Builder is a one-stop shop for creating great-looking, customized web-up forms to attract subscribers and turbo-charge sales. This application is so easy, so creative, and so smart that you'll be hooked the first time you use it. It's completely visual, with drag 'n drop editor, 500+ form designs and dynamic "thank you" pages.

http://jaymaxmarketing.com/getresponse

KickStartCart – For a more advanced autoresponder for your clients KickStart is awesome. They offer a shopping cart, secure order forms, and a client database you can grow up to 10,000 without any additional charge.
http://jaymaxmarketing.com/kickstart

Domains

GoDaddy – If you have the Internet you have probably heard of GoDaddy before. They are one of the best domain name registrars in the world. If you follow this link you will get your domains at a cut rate. To get this special rate, make sure you are not signed into your GoDaddy account. Click the link and choose your domain. Follow it all the way through to the end (sign in or create an account when you are prompted) and at the very end you will see the discount applied just before you get your card charged. VERY IMPORTANT!!! When buying a domain from GoDaddy they are going to offer you a million other little products: hosting, email, etc. Hit NO THANKS on each of these things. GoDaddy is a great registrar but you don't need all their upsells.

http://jaymaxmarketing.com/godaddy

Header Creation

XHeader – I used to spend a lot of time messing around with Photoshop, now I hardly ever even open it because I have XHeader. This little program makes life so easy because it is set up with one purpose, creating great looking headers for your websites. They have a free version...

http://jaymaxmarketing.com/xheader with limited templates and a paid version with 5000 templates. Upgrade to the paid version and you will see that you really don't have to be a graphic artist to make amazing looking headers. http://jaymaxmarketing.com/xheaderpro

Hosting

BlueHost – CPanel hosting at its best!!! I have been using BlueHost for a while now and they are amazing. Their tech support really knows how to help you. Recently my main blog was completely wiped out. They had it restored in about 20 minutes. I love these guys. Their fee works out to be about $6.99 a month, but you will be charged for the entire year. So your card will be charged $83.88. This includes the hosting for unlimited domains and unlimited storage http://jaymaxmarketing.com/bluehost

(Do not buy any of the pro, or add on services)

HostGator – These guys also offer CPanel hosting and they are ok, there service isn't the best in my eyes. They also offer unlimited domains and storage. The one benefit with them is that they charge by the month instead of by the year. http://jaymaxmarketing.com/hostgator

FREE VIDEO*****Installing a blog – This is a free video that I created to show my students how to install Wordpress on BlueHost or HostGator
http://jaymaxmarketing.com/installwordpress

Incorporation

The Company Corporation – Ten years ago I found this company and used them to incorporate a consulting firm I owned at the time. They are still around and doing a great job for their clients.

If you want to incorporate your business I highly recommend these guys. http://jaymaxmarketing.com/incorporate

Merchant Accounts

iPowerPay -If you do business today you need the ability to accept credit cards. This is one of the best merchant account services in the world. They allow you to have terminals in your business and have them on websites as well. When I joined it was absolutely free and it only took them 24 hours to have me all set up to accept all the major cards http://jaymaxmarketing.com/ipowerpay

Mentoring Programs

All Access Pass – Get access to EVERY piece of training that I have ever created. Plus get access to me in live webinars, weekly teleseminars, and even by email and phone. PLUS get access to all the new things that I create. All for one low price. http://LocalBusinessMaximumResults.com/allaccess

More Training

Connie Ragen Green – Writes a **FREE** blog that you can read for free that tells all kinds of hints and tricks to become successful at marketing online. She is my number one mentor and a close personal friend.

http://jaymaxmarketing.com/connie

How To Become A Webmaster – Three hours to become your own expert. I do this by spelling out all the things you need to do to make a WordPress site Search Engine friendly. You will use this as a resource as you learn and develop your own website, no coding required. I still use all these techniques with my client's sites. http://HowToBecomeAWebmaster.com

Marketing Tutorials – Learn from the biggest experts in the world about how to make more money online. Learn the marketing techniques that are key to earning an income online. http://jaymaxmarketing.com/marketingtutorials

Facebook Ads Secret Training (F.A.S.T.) FaceBook, the fastest growing and largest Social Network in the world is poised to surpass ONE BILLION members. Are you ready to tap into this massive market? Chances are you're not...chances are you realize the potential and have already tried to crack that market but failed. If you follow the conventional training that's out there you WILL fail. Discover How To crack FaceBook...Click here Now... http://jaymaxmarketing.com/fast

CRAZY Facebook if you are looking for an amazing training course on facebook and don't have the money to spend on the one above. Take a look at this one. This course is designed by myself and facebook guru Sam Bakker. You will learn how to create fan pages, and FB apps which can go viral in days! http://fanpagesbyjason.com/crazyfacebook/

Armand Live – This is the event that changed my life. After going to this weekend in Atlanta, I knew that I could really make money online and be successful. Armand does these a few times a year and if you click on my link you can get a special price, saving almost $800 bucks!. You can also meet Connie Ragen Green and myself at the event. I hope to see you there. http://jaymaxmarketing.com/freepass

Niche Sites

Cookie Cutter Blogs (PRO)– get in on this special program where I create 100 residual income producing websites for you.

http://CookieCutterBlogs.com/pro

Password Management

RoboForm – Do you ever feel like you have too many passwords to keep up with? Well, once you start this business you will find that it seems like you are always creating new accounts and needing to memorize new passwords. Some people keep a file on their computer or a piece of paper. What if either of those go destroyed? For like $10 a year you can have an amazing solution. I use this thing twenty times a day at least. It is my favorite tool. This creates a toolbar on your browser window and when you want to open a password protected site you just click the drop down box and select the name of the site. It takes you to the site, fills in your username and password and logs you in. Quick fast and easy!
http://jaymaxmarketing.com/roboform

Social Media

TweetAdder – This is a program that I use every day to automate my tasks for small businesses that use Twitter. It allows me to get them a lot of followers in the local area and it allows me to tweet out massive amounts of messages to their followers with a click of a button. Awesome tool!
http://jaymaxmarketing.com/tweetadder

Social Media Marketing Explained – If you want an in depth study of how social media works for business take this course by Connie Ragen Green. This course is over four hours of video training. Connie has over 25,000 followers on Twitter and she knows how to monetize them. Great program. http://jaymaxmarketing.com/greensocialmedia

Technology

Cookie Cutter Blogs – If you are afraid that you are not going to be able to make a lot of money because you don't have the technical skills to create good looking, SEO friendly blogs for your clients. I have a short cut for you. I will personally create all the "back end" (the hard stuff) for your blog so that it is optimized for the search engines. Then I will give you a plugin (and train you on how to use it) so that you can simply clone the site I made over and over for new clients. All you will have to do is add their unique content all the hard work is done! http://CookieCutterBlogs.com

DropBox - This is a really cool tool that you can use. When you install it it puts a folder in your My Documents folder called DropBox. You can then connect with other people and give them permission to view/edit files within that folder. So they will be able to see your files and you can see theirs. Very cool and the best part is…its free! http://DropBox.com

FTP – If you need to move files back and forth between your computer and your website then you need an FTP (File Transfer Protocol) program. My favorite is called FileZilla and it is 100% free. Download it from this site right here http://JayMaxMarketing.com/ftpprogram

Easy Redirect Script – really cool way to take long links and shorten them. When I create an offer on Google Places for a client I always use Easy Redirect script to shorten the link. Then I can promote something that looks like this… "http://JayMaxMarketing.com/MyOffer" instead of…"http://maps.google.com/coupons/page?oi=lbc&did=0_2805 65&hl=en-US&gl=US"

This video explains how it works
http://jaymaxmarketing.com/easyredirectscript

Video Creation

Camtasia – This program allows you to do screen captures, add music, fancy transitions, and render it all for the web. I used Camtasia to create the video portion of this product. Wonderful piece of software that has a 30 day free trial. http://www.TechSmith.com

Animoto – Free site that lets you make some really cool videos with music set to it by simply dragging and dropping into an interface. It is really neat and clients love it. They have an upgrade for $5 a month that will give you a lot more functionality and allow you to make longer videos. For just a little bit more you can even have them create videos for you in HD (High Definition) http://jaymaxmarketing.com/animoto

Wordpress Themes

MarketersCMS – One of the most amazing themes for

Wordpress, designed by one of the world's greatest Internet marketers, Armand Morin. This theme allows you to make multiple opt-in pages for one site, it integrates all the payment processing systems, and it has tons of videos and help to make this virtually idiot proof. Watch the free video here http://jaymaxmarketing.com/marketerscms

Headway Themes – Offers a really cool Visual Editor that allows you to move things around on the screen with your mouse. You can resize areas, move around navigation, and do lots of other cool things. http://jaymaxmarketing.com/headwaythemes

Elegant Themes – Simple and elegant themes that offer a lot of functionality that clients seem to really like. You can choose from 30 different themes and use as many as you like for up to a year for one low price. (***Make sure you get an account for each client and pass this cost along to them!***) http://jaymaxmarketing.com/elegantthemes

OptimizePress - is a revolutionary new WordPress Theme that gives you the power to create killer squeeze pages, sales letters, one-time offer pages, launch pages and much more, all through a simple point and click interface. You don't need to be a technical genius, and you certainly don't need a graphics degree to create amazing looking and high converting pages with OptimizePress. We have literally leveled the playing field when it comes to Internet Marketing page creation tools, there is nothing on the market which is even half as powerful as this theme.

http://JayMaxMarketing.com/optimizepress

<u>Notes</u>

Notes

<u>Notes</u>

Acknowledgments

This book was written after a long time of wishing and wanting it to be done. Lots of people told me that I needed to share my secret techniques with the world. I knew they were right because so many companies have websites and so few of them really have a presence on the web. I felt a special need to help businesses, especially during this time of economic distress which is causing many businesses to close their doors forever. I would like to thank my family for sticking by me and believing in me despite all the times in the past that I have failed you. Mom, Tony, Michelle, Megan and others. I would like to thank all the people in my life who pushed me to greatness. Specifically, Connie Green you have been the light at the end of the tunnel for me. Also to the people that are in my coaching program. *You are all an inspiration to me.*

p.s. to find out more about my coaching, visit:

http://LocalBusinessMaximumResults.com/allaccess

www.ingramcontent.com/pod-product-compliance
Lightning Source LLC
Chambersburg PA
CBHW051525170526
45165CB00002B/606

* 9 7 8 1 4 6 3 7 6 7 3 1 0 *